I0187965

KEITH MITCHELL: THE MAN I KNOW

BY

Denis G. Antoine, PhD

Keith Mitchell: The Man I Know

Copyright © 2023 by Ambassador Denis G. Antoine, PhD

All rights reserved. No part of this publication may be reproduced, distributed, or transmitted in any form or by any means, including photocopying, recording, or other electronic or mechanical methods, without the prior written permission of the publisher, except in the case of brief quotations embodied in critical reviews and certain other noncommercial uses permitted by copyright law. For permission requests, write to the publisher, addressed "Attention: Publisher" at the email address below.

Ordering Information:
Quantity sales. Special discounts are available on quantity purchases by churches, associations, and others. For details, contact the publisher at the address below. Orders by U.S. trade bookstores and wholesalers. Please email: admin@aknowingspirit.com.

Dedication

This book is dedicated to all my predecessors who served in Grenada's early years of diplomatic representation; I thank them for their early efforts. It is also committed to those with whom I served as counterpart, in various jurisdictions.

It is especially devoted to present and future Grenadian envoys, with the hope they will see the need to leave trails for others to follow.

I wish to acknowledge the inspiration derived from many foreign nationals who have enlisted in the service of Grenada; embraced Grenada with goodwill, and contributed their expertise to benefit Grenada.

This book is also dedicated to my brothers and sisters, our wives, husbands, children and extended family who have motivated me and inspired my work in the service of Grenada.

CONTENT

"It is not the critic who counts; not the man who points out how the strong man stumbles, or where the doer of deeds could have done them better. The credit belongs to the man who is actually in the arena, whose face is marred by dust and sweat and blood; who strives valiantly; who errs, who comes short again and again, because there is no effort without error and shortcoming; but who does actually strive to do the deeds; who knows great enthusiasms, the great devotions; who spends himself in a worthy cause; who at the best knows in the end the triumph of high achievement, and who at the worst, if he fails, at least fails while daring greatly, so that his place shall never be with those cold and timid souls who neither know victory nor defeat."

- Theodore Roosevelt,
Speech at the Sarbonne
Paris, France
April 23, 1910

FOREWARD

On many occasions over the years, while in the service of Grenada, I have been approached by Grenadians wanting to know my opinion of Dr. the Rt. Hon. Keith Mitchell. The inquiries came as no surprise; it was always about, "I hear they say."

Since I have had the honor of serving Grenada under his leadership, I learned, and know good things about him. After reading the following poem, '*I Know Something Good about You*', by an unknown author, I decided to share my knowledge about the man I know.

> *"Wouldn't this old world be better,*
> *If the folks we meet would say.*
> *I know something good about you,*
> *And then treat us just that way!*
> *Wouldn't it be fine and dandy,*
> *If each hand clap warm and true,*
> *Carried with it this assurance*
> *I know something good about you!*
> *Wouldn't things here be more pleasant*
> *If the good that's in us all*
> *Were the only thing about us*
> *That folks bother to recall*
> *Wouldn't life be lots more happy*
> *If we would praise the good, we see*

For there is such a lot of goodness
In the worst of you and me
Wouldn't it be nice to practice
This fine way of thinking too,
You know something good about me,
I know something good about you!

My first call to the service of Grenada abroad was to stand as Counsellor/Alternate Representative at the Embassy of Grenada/ Permanent Mission to the Organization of American States (OAS) in Washington, D.C.

"Why would you put yourself in that?" I was asked by those familiar with the situation in Grenada. "Things are very unpredictable" they would say. Maybe they had a point, but the warnings didn't stop there.

"You better be careful," I was told. "You'll just be used and then pushed aside, because things are not stable," they cautioned.

I have asked myself why such impressions were conjured up by individuals who expressed interest in seeing Grenada move forward. For me, what was most disheartening about those interactions was the fact that no one was able to serve as a witness to the many negative warnings they espoused and freely passed along, leaving others to believe. It was always, "Ah, I hear they say."

There have been other amazements that caught me off guard, such as negative utterances about Mitchell's social class. Despite these sentiments, the man kept his focus on Grenada and the task of nation building.

Newly elected Prime Minister Mitchell addresses the Special Meeting of the Permanent Council of the Organization of American States, 1996

It was reassuring that among the small group establishing the structure of the early New National Party (NNP) Support Group in the Washington, D.C. area were carryovers from the Grenada National Party (GNP). Among the GNP supporters there was adulation when, as an effective young enthusiastic member of the NNP, Keith Mitchell stood with the Honorable Herbert Blaize—and when Blaize supported Mitchell in kind.

However, when it became necessary for more talent in the Party to arise; and Keith Mitchell emerged as the one who was able to frankly express the vision that NNP needed to be more futuristic, the true feelings of some members of the group were revealed. There were some objections to Mitchell's very transparent and impartial call on Herbert Blaize for more dynamism in his leadership.

When Blaize fell ill, and had to travel to Walter Reed National Military Medical Center in Washington D.C. for treatment; it became clear there was a rough road ahead in building consensus on the future leadership of the NNP. Most importantly on the national front at home and within the support group in Washington D.C., close associates of Blaize encouraged him to step aside. Ben Jones was thought to be the best alternative, but Ben would not challenge Blaize. The polls showed that Blaize would lose the upcoming election; however, Mr. Blaize became uneasy, because he felt his leadership was threatened. Support from close friends of Blaize was shifting to Keith Mitchell, who was encouraged to step up because there was a growing confidence in him to lead the Party. It came as no surprise that Mitchell was elected political leader at the convention. As a result, he was abruptly removed from his ministerial appointments, only to be supported later by members of Blaize's cabinet, bringing a split, creating the GNP, and the NNP.

At that time, the Washington D.C. Support Group was led by one of the closest duos of Mitchell. The group began to canvass the members in the DC area to determine where the membership stood in support of Keith Mitchell.

Other unexpected maneuvers against Mitchell came from perceived supporters. These included negative letter writing and attempts to shame Mitchell before Herbert Blaize—especially when he visited Washington D.C. to meet Grenadians in the diaspora at a Town Hall style meeting held at the Embassy of Grenada.

"Don't hide," Blaize would say, "Present it to me."

Credit has to be given to the late Hon. Herbert Blaize, who challenged anyone with evidence of wrong doing by Keith Mitchell to step up from the crowd. No one did; but attempts to discredit Mitchell continued.

Still, through it all, Mitchell kept his focus on delivering for the people of Grenada. The word "deliverables" became Keith's common theme. It's also worth noting that Mitchell was challenged to deliver the Office of Ambassador to a member of the Support Group, instead of Ambassador Mr. Albert Xavier, who was the choice of Blaize to head the Grenada Mission in Washington D.C.

Prime Minister Dr Keith Mitchell (lt.) visits the OAS Headquarters in Washington early in his first term as Prime Minister.

INTRODUCTION

When Keith Mitchell was sworn in as Prime Minister by Governor General, Dame Cécile La Grenade, following the NNP landslide victory on March 13, 2018, his remarks at the ceremony held in the Grenada Trade Center are worth pondering.

"I am humbled by your confidence in me, and the team you have chosen, but that is just the elected team, the real team is all of us," Mitchell articulated.

He also added that his first task would be to write a formal   letter inviting the National Democratic Congress (NDC)—the opposition party at the time; officially requesting their participation "in the interest of nation building."

"We do not have to fight each other every day of the year. This electoral war is over, let peace reign," Mitchell declared—acknowledging that in a democracy, people are entitled to support a party or group of their choosing. He went on to say that while the NNP had won overwhelmingly, still "this winner does not take all." He was determined to make a clear statement that his administration is to let all voices be heard in a profound way.

Mitchell told the nation that the victory would be meaningless if, after five years, Grenada could not lift more people out of poverty.

"We cannot build this nation if we leave out or marginalize people who do not share our view," he added.

What that victory statement reflected is consistency in character and resolve. Keith Claudius Mitchell is the longest serving Prime Minister Grenada has ever had. He has gallantly led the NNP, and he has led his people as Head of Government and as Opposition Leader. He was chosen by his peers and he has followed the wishes of his people. When he was Leader of the Opposition in Parliament, Keith Mitchell maintained constructive and informed engagement in the governance deliberations.

Dr. Cynthia Carter
Asst. Professor of Medicine
Harvard University
Boston
Massachusetts

Dear Sir,

I had been a visitor to your very special Island over the last few days and had the opportunity to meet, interact and socialize with many of your friendly people.

My visit here was of a professional nature as a member of Black American Psychiatric Association which decided to hold its Annual Convention in Grenada this year. I must say that their choice was an excellent one and although I had some apprehension based on what happened here in 1983 I enjoyed my stay thoroughly.

I am presently an Assistant Professor of Medicine at Harvard University in Boston, Massachusetts, having earned a Bachelor Degree from Howard University in 1984, I attended the University of Illinois Medical School in (1984-1988) and did my Internship at Yale University, specialising in the field of psychiatry.

Having been around, one can see that there is need for improvement in several areas. This is if we judge them on our North American standard, but these can certainly be overcome by a resilient people which appear to be the case.

This visit also had another positive result as I had the opportunity to meet one of my former professor at Howard University. I am talking of no . 'lesser' person than Dr. Keith Mitchell, who is now active in your local politics and who is a possible leader of your country.

I have little knowledge of your other leaders but I can say without any reservation that Dr. Keith Mitchell certainly demonstrated some serious characteristics of a leader, while he was at Howard University. It was in 1980 that I begun my BSC program and was told by my friends who were already there, that if you really want to learn Mathematics you must take Dr. Mitchell's classes. I was not disappointed, as I was immediately struck by his dedication, commitment thoroughness and patience in his classes. His concern for his students especially those from the disadvantaged class was immediately obvious. He kept urging all of us to work harder and believe in ourselves. His constant Theme was "The difference between success and failure for most of us is the level of effort expended." I must say that this went a long way in my success.

On three successive years Dr. Mitchell was voted by the students and Maths Department as the best Mathematics teacher at Howard. The entire Mathematics fraternity at Howard moaned his departure in 1983.

We lost not just a Mathematic teacher but a wonderful human being. I believe that our loss was your country's gain, and although I cannot tell Grenadians who to vote for, I believe that Dr. Mitchell must be one of the few with his intellect, . energy, experience, International Connections and the ability to get things done.

Sincerely,

Dr. Cynthia Carter
Asst. Professor of Medicine

Chapter One
Leadership for True Achievements

How many times have you wished that someone would have done something differently from the way it was done? Well, growing up in Grenada, it appeared that relying on gossip was how many received information and made decisions. As one would expect from a social environment such as this, it is easy to understand why generalizations about a person's character were often made without knowing the individual. You might hear someone say 'That is what makes *him* who he is...'. This is simply a convenient way to justify unsubstantiated gossip about others.

However, during Mitchell's 2006 Independence message, gossip could not undermine the strength and leadership shown in his heart-felt delivery. It was definitive. At the ceremony to commemorate Grenada's 32nd Anniversary of Independence on February 7, 2006, The Prime Minister articulated this message:

My fellow Grenadians, I greet you with a profound sense of pride as we celebrate another Anniversary of our Nation's Independence. Today is a day to reflect on the bold and courageous steps taken by our Founding Fathers who

3

paved the way for our accomplishments during the last thirty-two years.

Today is also a day to thank God for the strength, and resilience that He has given to Grenada and its people and to acknowledge the many blessings and benefits He has bestowed on us. Let us offer up to Him our dutiful praise and thanksgiving.

Sisters and brothers, we have gained our independence but in actual fact, have become more interdependent and more interconnected with the rest of the world. This was demonstrated when our Caribbean family, and our friends and supporters from outside the Region willingly came to us in our time of need, following the devastation from hurricanes Ivan and Emily.

Let us continue to express our appreciation for their prayers and assistance. Enough praise cannot be given to the Governments and people of the United States; Trinidad and Tobago; Guyana; all other CARICOM and OECS nations; Cuba; Venezuela; the United Kingdom; The People's Republic of China; Belgium and Canada and all others, for their assistance.

Similarly, enough praise cannot be given to those teachers, nurses and doctors; Public Officers; members of the private sector and community groups; utility workers; dock workers; farmers, the employees within the tourist industry and the many volunteers who eagerly gave of themselves under such difficult circumstances - many of whom continue to do so.

Sisters and Brothers, all of us recognize that the road ahead will not be easy. Each of us will have to make

4

additional sacrifices to safeguard our future and our children's future. Over the past few weeks there has been much debate about who should contribute to the National Reconstruction Levy and how much should be contributed.

I take the opportunity of this Independence Day Address, to publicly thank the many groups and individual citizens who sought to help Government bring clarity and understanding to this issue. In particular, gratitude is extended to the Grenada Chamber of Industry and Commerce; the Conference of Churches; the Grenada Hotel and Tourism Association; and the Employers Federation for their contribution to the process.

I would also like to thank the Trades Union Council for their part in the debate. I hope that in 2006 Government and the Trade union leadership can work closer together to move our country forward. In this regard Government is giving its full support to the continued dialogue with our social partners…Business and Trade Unions, mediated by the churches. Sisters and Brothers, self-reliance and self-sacrifice were admirable strengths of our forefathers, qualities we should continue to preserve.

Therefore, it is important for us to acknowledge that while we appreciate the help of our friends, in the final analysis, we must accept fully the responsibility to help ourselves. Grenadians must continue to work together and make the necessary efforts and the vital sacrifices that are needed to take this beautiful Country forward on a sustainable basis. During the past decade, we have made many strides as a people. In the process, we faced setbacks yet we maintained

5

our course. We have worked hard to move our Country forward.

We have received commendation for our united efforts from many international organisations. The United Nations Development Programme (UNDP) Human Development Index is now ranking Grenada higher than ever before. We have moved from position number 93 in 2004 to 66 in 2005. Eastern Caribbean Central Bank Governor, Dr. Dwight Venner, recently called us a model for recovery and rebuilding. The International Monetary Fund Directors wrote to their membership telling them that the Government and People of Grenada must be commended highly for our response to the rebuilding of Grenada.

Sisters and Brothers all, let us on this Independence Day, be proud of our achievements...Let us be proud of one another and proud of our Country. Let us thank God for these and other achievements. Let us thank God for his mercy and thankful that we have lived to see another year of our country's independence. Let us thank God for the progress this country has made in the regional and international arena.

Let us thank the Almighty for peace and stability; let us thank God for the continued growth of our tourism industry and for the redevelopment and improvement of our hotels, the cruise terminal and other developments within the industry, which will see it grow even further. Let us thank God for the rebirth of our agricultural industry and the fact that we are now self-sufficient in many of the crops that we were importing at this time last year.

Let us thank God for the continued improvements in

6

our roads, bridges and our infrastructure in general. Let us also thank God for those who have made us proud. Our sportsmen and women like Alleyne Francique, Hazel Ann Regis, Devon Smith, Rawle Lewis, Jason Roberts and others. For the bravery of Private Beharry; Gratitude must go to Sir Royston Hopkin and his team for our new Five Star Hotel, the first of its kind in Grenada and indeed to all other hoteliers who are making serious sacrifices to rebuild; to the many leaders who have been working tirelessly as volunteers on various community development projects including disaster management and the many students who have made us proud. The list goes on.

Sisters and Brothers we should also at this time thank God for giving us the wisdom to accept criticism for our shortcomings and the strength to make corrections. Given the limited natural resources and the complexity of problems that continually surface for Small Island Developing States like Grenada, in education and human resources, particularly in the young, is extremely worthwhile.

An educated society is not only the best hope for maintaining democracy, but is also the best and cheapest way for small countries like ours to fashion and maintain free, fair and just societies. Experts in the USA claim that for every dollar they spend on education and youth development, they get five dollars in return.

In this regard, your Government has led the way in prioritizing youth development. Over the next few months we expect to launch our National Youth Service, which will provide training and jobs for thousands of our children.

This initiative, along with other youth programmes like our extremely successful scholarship drive, will greatly improve the lives of our children and help to create a better society. We have also invested heavily in the productive sectors. We will continue to provide incentives and financial help for our agriculture and business sectors.

We also expect to continue providing meaningful services and assistance to our most vulnerable citizens, including housing assistance, bus fares, books, school meals and uniforms support for our most vulnerable children. We are also providing an increase in Old Age Pension. Sisters and brothers, let us on this day pledge to create a better Grenada, Carriacou and Petit Martinique, in keeping with your Government's long term vision for a healthy, educated, productive and prosperous Nation. I have observed with very keen interest the number of Grenadians who have been proudly displaying our flag on their houses, vehicles and so on. This is the kind of nationalistic spirit and pride we need all year round not only at independence. Grenada must be first for the sake of our children.

In this same nationalistic spirit, let us all embrace the theme for 2006 'Independence - Promoting growth, stability and poverty alleviation' - today and every day of the year.

Indeed, sisters and brothers, let us dedicate ourselves to the preservation and improvement of democracy and to the education and development of our children. Let us work together to stamp out the deadly evils of crime and drugs. And let us continue to work with our international partners to defeat terrorism.

Let us resolve to show more compassion and generosity to the poor and needy. Let us also give our best in whatever we do and in whatever circumstances we find ourselves. Finally, in the words of my favourite hymn, Bread and Wine "For our Brothers Lord we do pray, For our parish Lord we do pray, For our Country Lord we do pray." "Happy Independence Day everyone, and may God bless our Nation."

In that speech Prime Minister Dr. Keith Mitchell addressed the people's welfare, spoke about inclusiveness and showed gratitude, hope and expectancy with confidence.

***

The records show that in the history of democratic governance in Grenada since attaining Independence in 1974, six men have been elected in national elections and appointed Prime Ministers of Grenada. Three men served as appointed interim Prime Ministers; one imposed as Prime Minister after the coup in 1979. The order of service and duration of terms are listed below:

The Hon Dickon Mitchell, (2022---) democratically elected

The Dr. The Right Hon. Keith Mitchell - (2018 – 2022), democratically elected

The Dr. The Right Hon. Keith Mitchell -

(2013 – 2018), democratically elected

The Hon. Tillman Thomas - (2008 – 2013), democratically elected

The Hon. Keith Mitchell - (1995 – 2008), democratically elected

The Hon. George Brizan, MP (1995), appointed caretaker

The Hon. Sir Nicholas Brathwaite (1990 – 1995), democratically elected

The Hon. Ben Jones (1989 – 1990), appointed caretaker

The Hon. Herbert Blaize (1984 – 1989) democratically elected

Mr. Maurice Bishop (1979 – 1983), Coup D'état self-imposed

The Hon. Sir Eric Gairy (1974 – 1979), democratically elected.

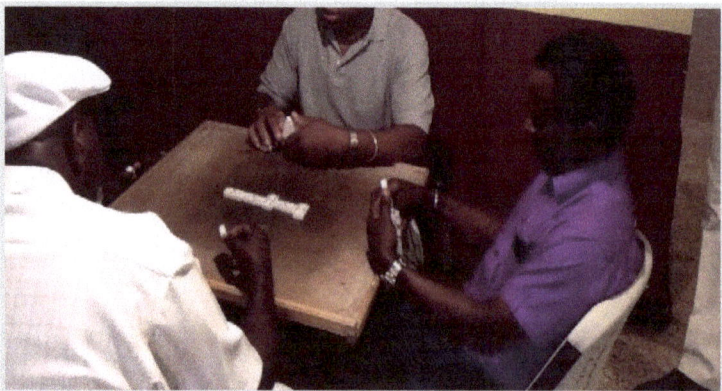

PM Mitchell enjoys a game of dominos in a NY basement.

There is a saying among Grenadians, *'That's the way he/she is.'* This saying could be interpreted to mean that one accepts his brothers and sisters and friends the way they are. However, sometimes these statements have unexplained connotations without knowing enough about a person.

And then comes the familiar refrain: *'Well, how he change so...he is not like his old self..."*

Statements like these only prove it is difficult to grow up and become the person you want to be. However when one does, there are always those who sneer.

Now don't get me wrong, I am merely bringing your attention to the fact that there is always a conversation going on about our national leaders and representatives. There is a culture of castigating public officials—which in too many cases, are careless and baseless.

Yet, so many times we see in others only what we are told to look for. We do not stop to examine for ourselves before forming conclusions. Grenadians seem to be habitually distracted by a culture of chinwag, and miss the truth and brilliance about each other.

Too often the humanity in each other is disregarded because of the usual typecasts in our

11

society, which support a tendency to hurl or label others by what we are told or overhear.

After almost fifty years as an independent nation, it seems appropriate and timely for Grenadians, at home and in the diaspora as one people, to reflect and celebrate the achievements and contributions of each other. We must applaud those who have, and are engaged in national leadership or serve well in public offices.

Prime Minister Mitchell, (rt) listens,
Amb. Antoine (lt), at American University
Washington D.C.

The unselfish commitments by Grenadians and other nationals who have presented themselves for public scrutiny to serve by relentlessly engaging in the struggle to contribute, promote and achieve continuous development, must be duly recognized. Any effort made by public and private officials toward improving the lives of others should earn our respect. Those efforts must be encouraged, respected and praised.

Having had the special honor and privilege to represent Grenada as ambassador for many years in several capacities, I have often been asked about our Grenadian heroes. It has become clear that in Grenadian society, there seems to be no clear consensus regarding our national stars. Our Olympian, Kirani James, has carved an indelible notch in Grenada's 21st century sports history, and will always loom large. Never forgetting the pace setter for Grenadian track and field athletes, Alleyne Jeremy Francique, who is a two time world indoor champion 2004 and 2006 winning his first world medal in 2003.

"It seems very easy for the nation to embrace our Olympian, for there was none before him. He will remain our first Olympian Gold Star," said then Prime Minister Keith Mitchell. But now we must hail and embrace Anderson Peters, Grenada's world champion javelin thrower.

Grenada must be proud to have nurtured such talent and provided the environment that facilitated and inspired the efforts that molded the character of our sports champions. It is well known

13

that our country has produced other world-class contributors in multiple fields. Grenadians never hesitate to lay claim and boast of the Mighty Sparrow, Mr. Killa and other Grenadian entertainers as Caribbean and global cultural icons who give us all bragging rights. I now present Keith Claudius Mitchell as a Grenadian political hero.

It is well established that in the game of cricket a hat-trick occurs when a bowler dismisses three batsmen in successive deliveries. Well, one might say, having mastered the art of cricket, Keith Claudius Mitchell is the only Grenadian and Caribbean constitutional leader to have dismissed his political opponents in free and fair national elections—15-0 seats on three occasions. Certainly, it goes without saying, that Keith is a national hero —having almost scored a *political* hat-trick. While that alone could solidify his standing as one of Grenada's political heroes, there is something else that should not go unnoticed. Mitchell's pattern of election and re-election as Prime Minister, demonstrates the country's confidence and trust in his leadership, especially when facing serious national challenges.

A stranger observing Keith Mitchell's deportment, as he was seen mingling with young constituents dubbed him, "A local man and a neighborhood brother."

I agree, he is our native son, husband, father,

now mature statesman, and celebrated longest-serving former Prime Minister of Grenada. Keith Mitchell pays attention to his people, whenever he is approached. He seems to treat everyone as the most important person he has ever met.

For many years, I have had the special privilege to walk with him, to learn and serve, always watching, as he presses on. Keith Mitchell is a man I have come to know beyond politics. I have seen that he continues to push on for the greater good. Keith Claudius Mitchell, the man, has built a strong legacy of unselfish professional, national and personal accomplishments in service to the land he loves and to humanity. Keith Mitchell is a Grenadian hero who's indelible impact on the nation will remain positive for generations to come. He will be counted among the citizens who have inspired and led the most measurable social progress in Grenada, since self-governance and Independence.

***

His quest for continued development of Grenada, Carriacou and Petite Martinique, his work will never go unnoticed—even by his detractors. When celebrating Dr. the Rt. Hon. Keith Mitchell, his dedication to Grenada and

Caribbean unity, his humility as a private citizen, his drive as a public servant and his commitment as a national and regional leader, are well acclaimed. He is a man who never allows his identity to be defined by the office he holds. We are reminded that 'great leaders don't allow their profession to become their identity'.

Keith Mitchell remains in touch with local, regional and global issues. He will engage with world leaders and remain consistent in his call for assistance for Grenada as one of the first lines of conversation—always remembering to say thank you, and often, remembering exactly what support Grenada has received over the years from the country he engages. He seems to have the memory of an elephant. It is significant to note that when he traveled as Prime Minister Mitchell, he was always well briefed on pertinent issues of the jurisdictions he visited and possible encounters he might have. Keith C. Mitchell, an unassuming man, of modest beginnings, entered public life with a determination rooted in a desire to succeed. And from the onset, he became known as a hard worker.

As a student at the Presentation Brothers College in Grenada, he excelled in mathematics and athletics. As a school teacher, he went beyond the call of duty to help his pupils. Keith is driven, passionate, has grit and shows perseverance in his approach to things. More importantly, he celebrates others.

He relishes success, but even when he would admit that it hurt to have lost the election to Dickon Amiss Thomas Mitchell, on June 23, 2022 there is something in him that gravitates to success. To see Keith Mitchell smiling and embracing the winner of the 2022 general election does not surprise me, because that is who he is.

***

To me, it is obvious that Keith Mitchell accepts his calling with a disposition of selflessness, void of aggrandizement, but with consistent strong self-confidence and excellent timing on when to be assertive. Unlike many others who have the desire to lead but thrust themselves with arrogance on the national scene—as if entitled to leadership more than others; Keith Mitchell entered the nation building movement with a sense of unpretentiousness. The way he offered himself for national service demonstrated that he understands the will of his people and possesses a common touch that signifies he is unlike too many politicians who seem to place themselves above average citizens.

Chapter Two
Responding to the Call for Action

Most Grenadians now know that Keith Mitchell gained early national recognition as he became and remains a first-class sportsman representing Grenada as our national cricket captain. He earned the respect of neighboring islands because of his personality and skills, which prepared him for the call to the Windward Island team to provide regional leadership.

He has maintained a passionate love for his childhood game, cricket. His studious application of himself is revealed even when he plays a wind-ball game on a safe closed street, which he enjoyed as a boy, and still plays like a boy even today. Distinguishing him from the boys in the game is only noticeable by his command stance at the wicket and when he is about to set the field for his bowling.

Keith Mitchell's relentless efforts to promote cricket as a strong unifying Caribbean cultural force of collective representation still endures. In North America, as a student and later as a successful consultant, Keith Mitchell became a leading proponent and activist in the movement to bring attention to Cricket in North America. His advocacy has had a major impact on elevating the North American Cricket league.

Prime Minister, in white t-shirt, enjoys his favorite sport on a safe street with children.

There is special admiration and support that lingers in the Caribbean diaspora in North America for Keith Mitchell. Among his most ardent supporters, are the families of Caribbean nationals with whom he maintains contact and closely communicates when traveling, notwithstanding his busy schedule. He often expresses regrets about not being able to reconnect when he is abroad because of scheduling.

In the annals of West Indian Cricket and the evidence of the sport as a uniting force in the Caribbean; Keith Mitchell is well respected for his contributions. He is appreciated, not only for his passion for the game of bat and ball, but for his wise counsel, which is regularly sought at the highest levels of the administration of the game, to help restore the glory that this West Indian game once reached. Dr. Mitchell's love for sports, in general, is well documented locally, regionally and nationally.

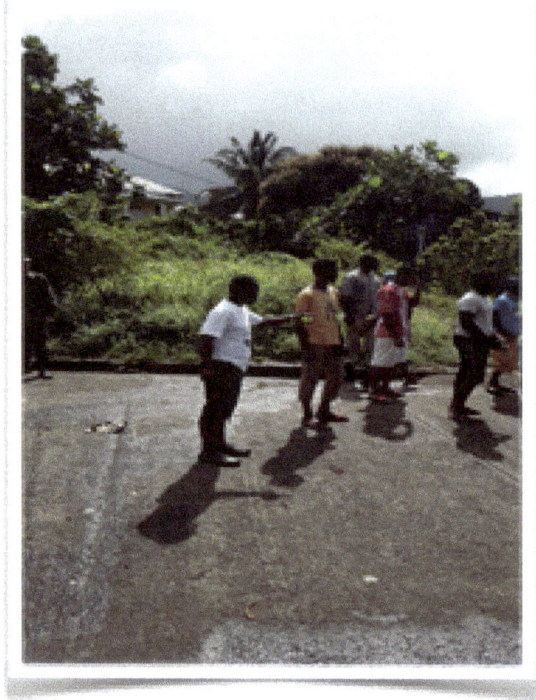

Then Prime Minister Keith Mitchell shows
leadership by action.

It is refreshing to see the Rt. Hon. Keith C. Mitchel playfully enjoying a game with the children; a simple moment reminiscent of his childhood. But through the game, the importance of displaying the proper decorum and sportsmanship is reinforced. This is another way he motivates and inspires youths.

It is obvious that his passion for sports, and his adulation of the Grenadians who have excelled in sports, have stirred the explosion of interest among Grenadian children in sporting activities. Keith Mitchell is an educator and he believes in education. More than that, he is a teacher. While he was Leader of the Opposition in Parliament, he made time to tutor students in his favorite subject, Mathematics. I won't be surprised when he publishes a math book, as he once proposed, because figures and calculations are in his blood. He repeatedly said he wants youths to love math and statistics.

***

The successive successful administrations of government led by Mitchell are testimony of his steadfastness. His enthusiasm for sports and promotion of a healthy lifestyle raised the level of interest in athletics among the youths of Grenada. Much of the groundwork related to outstanding sporting policies and facilities in Grenada is a direct reflection of his consistent elevation of athletics as part of the national development agenda.

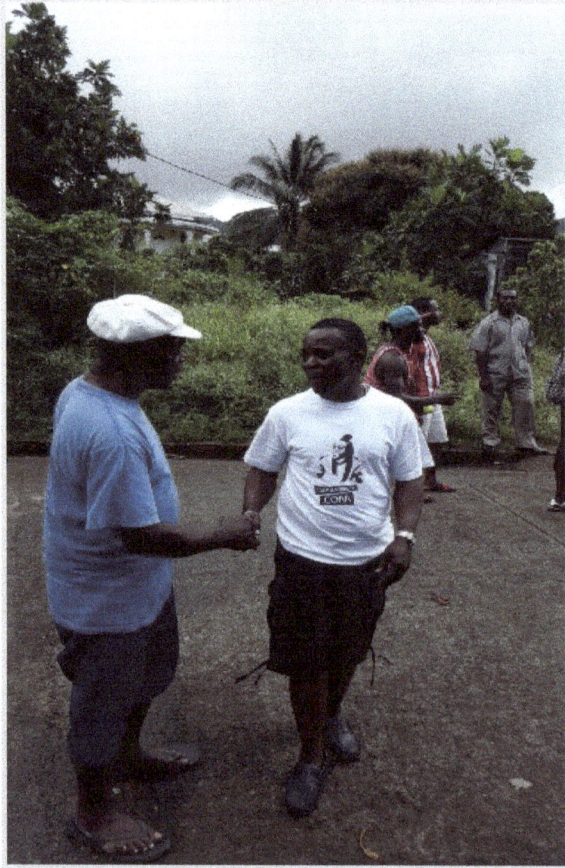

Prime Minister Keith Mitchell enjoys his favorite
sport and pauses to greet constituencies.

He has continuously espoused that sports is a critical component of healthy and holistic development. On August 31, 2017, as Prime Minister of Grenada, Dr. Keith Mitchell lauded Caribbean athletes who participated in the IAAF World Championships in Athletics, and the World Para Athletes Championships in London.

"As chairman of CARICOM, I take this opportunity to recognize all the athletes from Caribbean nations who participated in the World Championships and who brought the attention of the world to our region," Dr. Mitchell wrote in his statement.

"The entire Caribbean is extremely proud of your performances in London particularly the Trinidad and Tobago Men's 4&400m Relay team which upstaged the United States as champions of the event for the first time since 2003," he added.

Dr. Mitchell also noted the accomplishment of Akeem Stewart of Trinidad and Tobago who set a world record in the Javelin at the World Para Athletics Championships in London, which preceded the World Championships. These remarks demonstrate his keen attention to sports in CARICOM.

Evidence of Keith Mitchell's abiding admiration of excellence in all categories of life skills, was exhibited when he took time to extend best wishes to Usain Bolt, as he was transitioning away from track and field. Moreover, he expects CARICOM to announce at a future date the deserving recognition to Bolt and other athletes who have made a significant contribution to sports. Dr. Mitchell has said that the success of our athletes reinforces the importance of sports tourism as a viable pillar of economic development to the region.

Dr. Keith Mitchell has a long record, well outlined and discussed, regarding the high value he places in sports. He promotes sports tourism, and the economics of sports. It is historic that Grenada hosted world cup cricket games. Despite efforts to discourage him, with disparaging words by opposition voices to frustrate his effort, the people of Grenada will not forget that because of his untiring efforts the game flourished in Grenada and the Caribbean.

He made major contributions to sports in the Caribbean Community, including successfully hosting the 2007 ICC World Cup along with other countries, and the 37th Match, Super Eights, ICC World Cup match which was played in St. George's, April 10, 2007. And that was one in a series of games to follow, based on Mitchell's persistence.

By his personal commitments—not only to regional sports, but as Prime Minister of Grenada, Keith Mitchell demonstrated a firm commitment to

26

embracing and strengthening provincial institutions. Another great example of regionalism is his support for the Caribbean Court of Justice (CCJ).

His efforts to amend Grenada's Constitution by the required referendum have been interpreted by him as learning opportunities and the maturing of the Grenada electorate. However, his call for removing contentious politics from issues requiring national consensus is another example of his unselfish leadership focused on careful reforms.

Chapter Three
Embracing the Call to Serve

Keith C. Mitchell's early entry into national politics revealed a somewhat prophetic call to service, which can be interpreted as a dedication of one's life to a greater calling. When he left home to study abroad, he seemed to have been listening to a voice of service to Grenada resonating deep within him.

It is reassuring to watch how he embraces and interacts with Grenadians at all levels and stations in life. Wherever and whenever he meets them, in Grenada or abroad, he is at home with his people. For instance, he will meet with people in their homes—often to the amazement of protective service. He is simply at ease among Grenadians and Caribbean nationals abroad in their milieu.

*Keith Mitchell while visiting as Prime Minister
paused for photo with Greg, and Liba after church
service in Brooklyn, NY.*

The history of the elected Prime Ministers of Grenada, since our Independence shows that there is an element of inspiration derived from the fact that most of our Prime Ministers travelled and looked at Grenada from abroad. While they worked, they all took action to return to the national arena of politics.

In the case of Keith C. Mitchell, the call to service was revealed while he was a college student at home in Grenada. Keith Mitchell remained steady and excelled in his personal and professional growth. He moved from The University of the West Indies (UWI), where he earned his bachelor's degree, to the United States of America.

Even while he found tremendous personal and professional success in business, while studying and working as a statistician, consultant, professor and even in the real-estate business; he kept focused and wrapped in the cause of Grenada, Carriacou and Petite Martinique. He seemed to find even more success serving others in the diaspora, which drummed up his urge to return home. Starting from the beginning of the 1980's—while many Grenadians talked, worried, and tried to escape the turbulence that was shaking Grenada, Keith Mitchell spoke up from North America about the grim situation at home. Still believing more could be done, he grew restless and knew he would eventually return home to serve.

Since meeting Keith Mitchell, I have observed his healthy desire to succeed. He notably brings a sense of urgency to the entire task. It began with his matriculation at the prestigious Howard University in Washington, D.C., eventually becoming a senior college professor in the field of Mathematics and Statistics. He could have stopped there, but remained riveted by the turmoil at home and heard the call to return.

Prime Minister Keith Mitchell praises the good work of civil servants at emulation ceremony.

Students and professional colleagues alike refer to his tenure at Howard University as outstanding—particularly because he went out of his way to assist others. Keith extended himself, realizing that among those with whom he worked abroad in the diaspora, were Grenadians and Caribbean nationals. He also reached out and worked collaboratively with many American citizens and friends, who shared his vision for Grenada. He was never self-absorbed, remaining preoccupied with how things were moving in Grenada. He went out of his way to ease the burden for others— making sure to reach out to his co-workers and friends.

The privilege to work closely with Keith Mitchell provided unmatched opportunities to observe him as he travelled about, when he studied and worked in the United States for almost 11 years. He was among a cluster of Grenadians who studied and worked in the Washington Metropolitan area and travelled along the Northeastern coast of the USA and up to Canada. He was recognized as he entered the community of Caribbean nationals in the diaspora, at a time when the Caribbean diaspora concept of working together began to emerge.

He became immersed in matters related to the national politics of Grenada from abroad, together with a core group of motivated

Grenadians. In the Washington D.C. area, as the situation in Grenada became inflamed, the relevance of Keith Mitchell's involvement became more noticeable. He networked with the centers of influence for CARICOM, the OECS in Canada, New York and Washington D.C., with his desire to calm the rising chaos in Grenada that had intensified. Mitchell's emergence as a leading voice in a growing Grenadian and Caribbean Community in the Washington Metropolitan area became well recognized. He had the attention of the circles of influence for whom he provided professional consultancy.

He stood up in a leading role of the Support Group in the struggle to bring back democracy and stability in Grenada, tension and instability mounted during the period of disintegration, of the Grenada revolution. Dr. Keith Mitchell stands out as pragmatic and results-oriented in his engagements. In the national organizations which were founded, he was action-oriented and that caught my attention. He promoted Grenada's and the Caribbean's interests as the diaspora sentiments rose.

His deep-rooted self-confidence, demonstrated with a sense of humility, is admirable. During 1972 through to 1983 Grenada, was at that time, among the subject of politics most discussed in homes in the Caribbean region and especially the diaspora communities in the USA.

He exhibited courage at a time when it was very unpopular and unsafe for a Grenadian to speak openly—even objectively and constructively about the many disquieting signals emanating from a deteriorating revolution. When the crisis could not be contained, Keith Mitchell was a leading voice in what was known as the Grenada Democratic Movement (GDM) in North America.

At the height of his personal and professional successes—which included the attainment of a PhD from the prestigious American University, as well as a growing portfolio of investments, Dr. Keith Mitchell risked everything and made the unselfish decision to return in 1983, during some of the darkest days in Grenada's political history.

Before his return, at that tumultuous phase, he became the leader of a group of concerned Grenadians in the Washington D.C. area that formed a party Support Group. The focus, at the time, was on the work of GDM, which was active in Canada, New York, and the Washington Metropolitan area. At the peak of the crisis in 1983, he travelled to Grenada, and amid the turmoil, narrowly escaped being nabbed.

He was forced to leave Grenada, but would

soon return, after briefing North American supporters. Yet, he remained immersed and restless about what was happening in Grenada. He intensified his call to action and began to raise attention about the festering situation at home.

***

Before leaving for Grenada, he led rallies on the street and parks in Washington, D.C; seeking support for Grenada. He returned in the wake of the demise of the revolution in the last quarter of 1983, at the height of his professional achievements.

As the USA intervention into Grenada abated, Dr. Keith Mitchell sustained his active role in the frustrating course of economic recovery, and resuscitation of the social and political health of the of the tri-island state. In the interim, leading up to the first national election, immediately after the failed revolt, he stayed in touch with the Support Group in the Washington, D.C. area. A call came from him to position the Support Group, as the New National Party (NNP) Support Group, elevating the group's functions to cheerleaders of an unfolding new phase in the return to democratic governance.

The task of reconstructing democratic institutions began and a new era in Grenada's

36

politics ensued. Dr. Keith Mitchell returned again to the US briefly, to provide updates on the situation at home, with reference to the formation of a union with the GDM, GNP (Grenada National Party) and other groups. After a series of meetings and negotiations on Union Island, the hybrid New National Party (NNP) emerged.

Mitchell's outlook on national politics was centered on creating harmonious engagement for the national good. At a meeting convened at his home in Maryland, before embarking on the journey to Grenada, Mitchell was asked about taking leadership on the national front.

"My interest is service," he said. "The country needs us, and I am not concerned about leadership now; to serve is most important."

It was at that point when he introduced Dr. Francis Alexis, another prominent Grenadian, who had articulated interest in national leadership, and Keith Mitchell offered to work with whoever was ready to commit to national unity. Dr. Keith C. Mitchell's actions then, reminded me of Kelly Miller, who said: "All truly useful men must be, in a measure, time servers, for unless they serve their time, they can scarcely serve at all." Keith Mitchell has been serving and continues to serve Grenada well.

Chapter Four
A Legacy of Getting Down and Lifting Up

The recorded history of modern Grenada shows that Dr. the Rt. Hon. Keith C. Mitchell has been serving Grenada continuously and courteously as a Member of Parliament since he was elected in 1984, and has served as Prime Minister longer than any other Prime Minister.

The legacy of many successful people has been associated with financial wealth. However, Keith Mitchell's legacy will be, in part, measured for his ability to 'get down' with his people—not to wallow, but to lift them up, lift their spirits and feelings about themselves, while also inspiring their hopes for a better life. Keith Mitchell listens with empathy and is solution oriented. He exhibits confidence and believes in people regardless of their station in life. Understanding that wisdom can come from anywhere, Keith has been known to revisit topics discussed with constituents, days or even months, after a casual exchange. Popularly referred to as 'Doc' by many, he is a genuine man of the people.

He questions with reason and has high expectations of those whom he embraces. There is toughness about Keith Mitchell, which is a gift. He is resilient, which is manifested by his commitment to continuous self-improvement.

To watch Keith Mitchell mix and mingle dexterously—at ease with himself, his peers, classmates and friends, is remarkable. In fact, his interpersonal dexterities are exhibited with people at all levels.

He is a cautious man that uses higher operation thinking skills. Keith looks at all sides—not just what is placed before him, but carefully considers several outcomes of a particular course of action.

Among his colleagues, in his capacity as Chairman of the Heads of Government of CARICOM, he commanded the respect of his peers. People turn to him for advice and good counsel, as he continues to prove that experience never grows old.

The fact that he gives full recognition to the need for leadership at all levels is admirable. He appreciates those who use their talents, skills and authority well. He has been patient and worked at all levels in his ascent to national leadership. As a result, he espouses that there is dignity in all forms of labor.

He has shown respect for national leaders who came before him; he studies their contributions and gives honor to their service. Yet, he reminds us that the past teaches while the future expects more of us. He understands his people and their behaviors when they are self-focused or vested in the community.

Keith Mitchell challenges those whom he engages, and like a teacher and professor, has become an excellent judge of character. He leads with authority.

He has grown to become more than a Grenadian, but a Caribbean and Commonwealth figure. He has done so in full view when he moved into the University of the West Indies (UWI) Barbados campus in 1968; where he remained actively engage in the UWI Community. His classmates and colleagues celebrate him today. Keith Claudius Mitchell has strong support and friendships from within the Caribbean region and beyond.

This trust and confidence in his regional stance for a united Caribbean Community has been exhibited, not only because he is recognized as the man to-go-to, for a good cricket match, but also during a tense time of socio-political turmoil in Guyana. It was Keith Mitchell's leadership as a voice of reason and consensus builder, that was called upon to mitigate that crisis. Today, there is admiration and respect from within the CARICOM, and in the global community.

Chapter Five
Effective Representation Abroad

Keith Mitchell is comfortable when he travels abroad, whether he is in the global spotlight or among Grenadians and other Caribbean people.

PM addresses 69th Session of the United Nations General Assembly

His voice reverberates as he addresses the United Nations General Assembly. A long queue is formed to greet him, with positive comments about his eloquent and hopeful message. Following his

43

presentation of the Nation's business at the UN, he did not miss the opportunity to converse with former classmates and friends in the margin of the UN annual meetings.

I recall his conversation with the Delegation of Iraq, when he paused on the floor of the UN General Assembly in September 2015. It was one of the most bold and candid chats I have witnessed. Speaking to the Leader of the Delegation of Iraq, the Prime Minister expressed his sympathy for the continuous loss of lives in Iraq and asked boldly when action will be taken to stop all the killing.

Mitchell engaged with the delegation and went on to ask pertinent questions about how Small Island Developing States (SIDS) could help in bringing an end to the violent situation in that country. He displays global and cultural competence. As a leader, he is at ease away from home, in much the same way he is at home.

***

Great value is assessed in the diaspora and Keith always expresses deep gratitude for such contributions. When he reaches out to Grenadian and Caribbean nationals while traveling to New York and the Washington Metropolitan areas, Mitchell makes sure to never forget the friendships that provided support and inspiration throughout his career. He returns to their homes to eat with them, to sit and talk, and to inquire about their children, families and friends. He stands face-to-face with the leaders of the world's largest democracies; he addresses issues pertinent to the family of nations; and he does so with competence and strategic timing. Dr. Mitchell has a very big intellectual appetite.

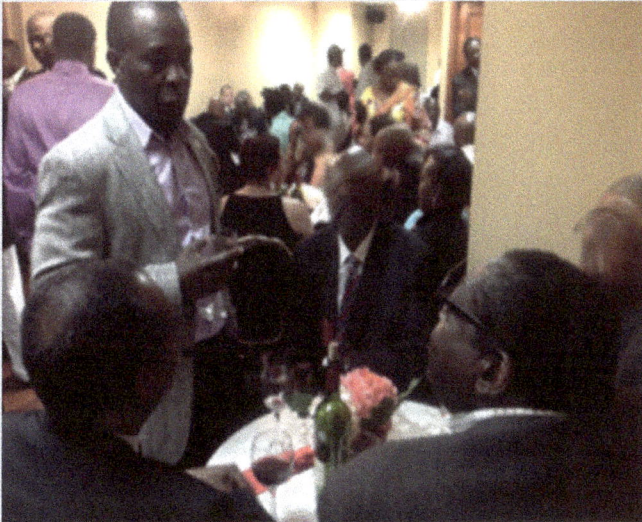

*Prime Minister chats with classmates
at a gathering in New York.*

Working with him requires that one's level of productivity be sustained. Whenever productivity

45

diminishes, Mitchell does not hesitate to send the message that low level output is not acceptable. Having *been* successful is not his interest. The question is: What more can be done? If yesterday's work still looks big, you have not done anything today.

Keith Mitchell expressed his camaraderie and concerns to the President of Nigeria with a benevolent smile. His guise and his headship reach can be disarming. He asked hard questions and expressed his concerns about troubling issues in Nigeria when he met with President Buhari at the United Nations.

It is refreshing to hear how he connects with world leaders, and the way in which he raises concerns about the troubling impact on SIDS. This, when the developed world is in conflict and unable to meet the obligations undertaken in international agreements. At the same time, Mitchell never neglects to express gratitude and appreciation for development and cooperation extended to Grenada.

As once the leader of a small country, the Rt. Hon. Keith C. Mitchell insists that small countries can have a big international impact. Yet, he seems to never lose his common touch—even while he maintains effective rapport with presidents and prime ministers, heads of state, ambassadors and representatives of the highest world order. Still, he returns to embrace the core citizens.

As a consummate envoy, he invites extended cooperation and is one of the most gracious hosts. When he received the Ambassador of the Republic of Turkey to the Caribbean, he was enthused by some 'welcomed' news of aid packages for Grenada, and he showed his appreciation.

After meeting the President of Turkey at the UN, it came as no surprise when His Excellency, Ambassador Aydin Evirgen, was appointed Ambassador to the Caribbean Community. At the opening of the Turkish Embassy in Santo Domingo, Dominican Republic, the Ambassador expressed to Prime Minister Mitchell that Turkey, through its International Development Agency, has committed to support several projects in Grenada.

As reported by the Grenada Information Service (GIS) on July 31, 2014, the projects included several very "urgent and necessary" fire trucks and an ambulance, to aid in the event of any disaster. Turkey also pledged to fully furnish or outfit five of our Nation's schools; provide tractors to aid in our agricultural development; and provide equipment for electrical testing and installation. Specific local initiatives in Information Communication Technology and Tourism were also supported by Turkey.

As a consummate diplomat, Prime Minister Mitchell welcomed Turkey's offer to work with

CARICOM countries, and fully fund for five years, a joint Embassy to advance both regions' interests. Dr. Mitchell welcomed Turkey's intent to appoint an Honorary Consul in Grenada. Turkey has signed a protocol agreement with CARICOM to establish a joint business council that would advance tourism and investments in the region. Prime Minister Mitchell, as a regional leader, readily conveyed his support to work along with his CARICOM counterparts, in enhancing relationships between CARICOM and Turkey. As Prime Minister, he also made sure to express his best wishes to Turkey for its 2014 campaign for a seat on the UN Security Council; and acknowledged Turkey's request for CARICOM's support.

The flexibility and ease in which Prime Minister Mitchell moves from stage to stage to address a diverse public, is an admirable leadership quality. He integrates well with the community—on the cricket field, in church, on the dominos table or at the cookout. He blends in among the people, and comports himself accordingly for each occasion.

The relationship between George Bush, the 43rd President of the United States, and Keith Mitchell was a most cordial one. They were co-chairs; President Bush, John Major of Australia and Keith Mitchell, as leaders of the International Democratic Union (IDU).

PM Mitchell & President George Bush,
43rd President of the US.

When Keith Mitchell and George Bush met there was an open and candid exchange. There was mutual respect and common concerns expressed on front line issues. Chief among the topics raised with President Bush, was the relationship with the Republic of Cuba and the need for more reliable and predictable engagement with the Caribbean. Mitchell reminded Bush about the positive contribution that people with Caribbean heritage make to the United States.

One cannot forget his bold decision in 1997 to lead a large delegation to the Republic of Cuba, during which historic agreements on sports, health and education were developed. His invitation to then President Fidel Castro was reciprocated the following year.

Chapter Six
Faith and Fellowship

At a church in Brooklyn, NY, the members were elated when the Prime Minister joined the service. Although the parishioners gave Mitchell special recognition, he insisted his participation was not as Prime Minister, but as a fellow member of the congregation and celebrant.

Sandra Antoine-Cato and PM Keith Mitchell

51

Look at the proud beam on my sister Sandra's face, and Keith's relaxed demeanor. He is not doing a favor, to pause for a photo, because of his office; he does not know who he is with, he is just genuine. My sister returned home from that church service after meeting Dr. Mitchell for the first time, and said, "The man is so nice, and real, he doesn't show off at all. He is just like one of us."

***

Keith is always there to support young people. He says the word "youth" so much, that it may be the reason he remains youthful! He takes every opportunity to teach and offer advice to those in their formative years. He understands the importance of mentorship and the wisdom that can come from people who went before you. In short, he never ceases to be "Teacher Keith".

His focus on skills training and youth development is supported by the energy he puts in personally contributing to the education of young people.

Generally, he views young people as the source of his existence. Similarly, he recognizes the contributions of village elders and working class people. He seems to draw strength from them as the root of his origin and receives them with honor and respect. Keith looks up to everyone. He places value in individuals regardless of their station in life. He is never hesitant to share a meal or a drink. Keith is like a member of the family.

One can tell when he feels comfortable in a setting, as he excels at sensing the nature of any situation. He listens, purposefully interacts, never flaunting or allowing his status to seem more important than anyone in his midst.

The smile on his face says, 'friend'. He embraces the smiles of others. He gives the impression that he is happy to be where you are, when in the present company. In step with helping youths, the words scholarship and training are always at the tip of his tongue—and he never spares a chance to push for scholarships for young Grenadians to study across the globe. He is a determined man whose actions are driven by his conviction to affect change. He flushes with passion for the education of young children. As a result, he has high expectations of persons in whom he places trust. At times, it can be difficult to keep up with him, due to his tireless efforts. In short, working with Keith Mitchell requires competence and confidence in one's abilities.

Through it all, he remains passionate and steadfast. Faith and family are the main pillars of Dr. Mitchell's being. He is a praying man. And those feelings of being swallowed up by the whale of character assassination were, indeed, a metaphoric revelation that his strength comes from his faith, and the support of family.

During his meeting with Pope Francis, there were several quiet moments of contentment that Keith once described as "unmatched." When I saw the smile on Dr. Mitchell's face that day, I wanted to ask jokingly what he confessed? He looked relieved and at ease with himself. It was a once in a lifetime moment. More importantly for Keith, a reminder of something he's always said: Faith will see him through.

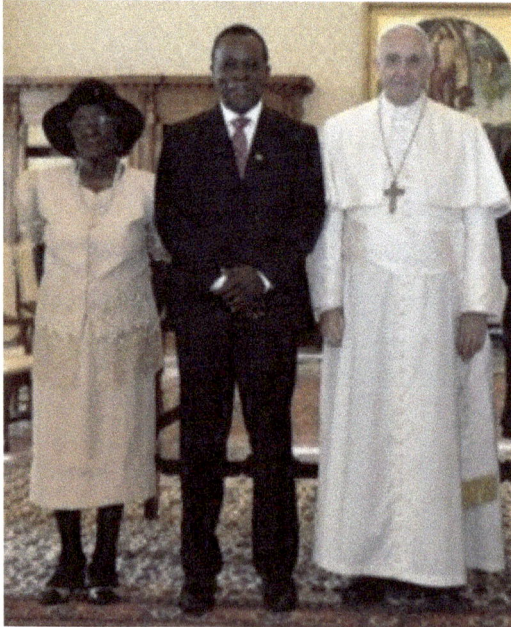

Prime Minister with his mother
and Pope Francis.

I remember being present when Keith Mitchell was speaking at a public meeting on the street in Happy Hill, when he recalled his Jonah like experience. Standing before his people, at a time when he was accused and ridiculed, then he seemed to grow tall and strong when he said to the people, "thank you for being here, I need your help."

It is that confidence in his people that Mitchell has also shown in himself, that's impressive. And it is that which separates him from other national figures.

***

At home and abroad, Keith is loved by his students and peers who regularly sing his praises. Whenever he returns to his alma mater, Howard University, he is welcomed with adulation. Keith is open about his experiences and happy to discuss his achievements to encourage his favorite audience— young people.

As a friend, he is trusting but always expects the best of you. He encourages and celebrates his friends. However, he is not afraid to express his feelings when he believes a person is wrong, or out of line. Nevertheless, when he agrees he will let you know.

Keith Mitchell loves action. He will not hesitate to remind you that talk alone does nothing. I recall him saying, "Well, what happen to you with this little, little, bit a thing? Past success is not enough."

He'd continue with, "That's why I am always driven to remain successful, to meet the people's expectations."

While it is not easy to please Mitchell, due to his high expectations, he remains grateful. He demands excellence and loves when people show initiative. Nevertheless, he appreciates consultation as a form of respect for his responsibility.

The Keith I know is trusting, until he is given reason to feel otherwise. He values privacy, and will not knowingly condone wrong. Keith listens without judgment, but relies on facts. He often says, "I won't make the same mistake twice."

He makes note of people's attitude toward him and others. Most importantly, he will passionately defend the rights of others.

He thinks about the future. "These children need our help…do something," he would say. So reasonably, his style is to appoint those who *can* do something. He never tells his team how to execute, but simply explains the need. Then he'd say, "You know what to do, you have the authority, you know your responsibility, and you know what the priorities of the government, and what the needs of the people are."

Connecting with students, farmers and others was part of his Face to Face outreach programs starting in 1996 that took him to villages, schools and community centers across the country where he listened to concerns and answered questions; eager to communicate and understand.

***

Direct actions on his part have been his assertive requests. For instance, on July 3, 2017, in the United Kingdom, Mitchell asked that the UK increase its quota of scholarships offered to students in Grenada and the rest of the Caribbean. He told the United Kingdom's High Commissioner to increase its quota of scholarships to Grenada and the region overall. This demand was particularly important in light of the UK's shifting immigration policy and benefits derived from our people.

His unifying ways allowed him to be embraced by the late Honorable Elvin Nimrod, who became a strong pillar of the NNP, and a much-admired colleague of Keith Mitchell.

He placed trust and confidence in Nimrod's contribution, which added to the success of the

NNP. Mitchell makes it clear that the importance of the people of Carriacou and Petit Martinique dictates his relationship with the Honorable Nimrod and because of his commitment to all of Grenada.

The accommodation of the Honorable Peter David into the NNP reflects Mitchell's critical thinking and long-term vision of his desire to transform the communal landscape and to ensure continued stability. He has been sending the message that the NNP is not only for its supporters that believe in the NNP, but also for those who need to be assimilated to enrich the NNP.

The success of the NNP depends on its values, and its ability to provide opportunities for all to enter the proverbial safe house—where the goal is to provide for the greater good of all. However, Mitchell reminds us that the NNP is not just for those who vote for the party, but serves as a symbol for all who desire to objectively contribute to building our nation. One must reflect for a moment on the character of Keith Mitchell—which has made all the difference. He has always been about selfless leadership and action, in order to benefit citizens of Grenada, Carriacou and Petit Martinique. For him, the mission has been about removing obstacles and making room to include all families.

He is at his best when visiting New York. He highly values the contribution of all Grenadians

58

abroad, but in New York the vibrancy of Grenadians in the 'Big Apple' resonates with him.

Dr. Mitchell's keen sense stands out in my mind. He recognizes the positive flows from Grenadians in NY—which includes a high professional development, levels of remittance, and in kind, contributions toward the development of Grenada.

He has been able to engage Grenadians in New York in a manner that encourages their collective effort to support Grenada in meaningful ways. He engages them with the understanding that one of the largest clusters of Grenadians abroad, cannot be overlooked. The results are clear. The impact of that engagement of Grenadians, and friends of Grenada based in New York on the national front is indisputable. Their contributions have led to sustained material and in-kind support for Grenada. As a result, Grenada is a home for trusted foreign nationals with decent character; and Mitchell is a most gracious host.

Keith Mitchell understands that New York is an extension of Grenada where much of the old traditions and Grenadian values are kept alive. The Grenadians who remain engaged also continue to have a measurable impact on our nation. The Prime Minister has high regard for the contribution and support of Grenadians in New York, and is open to opportunities that would demonstrate that

59

appreciation. Overall, he remains politically aware of the economic and enabling link between New York and Grenada, and all the other clusters of Grenadians in the diaspora.

***

"If I must do your job, why do I need you there?" Keith sometimes challenges.

Mitchell has prioritized being accessible and, as I mentioned before, promptly responds. He works with a sense of urgency. "Let's get that done," he would say. Followed by, "how soon?"

When Keith Mitchell believes in an individual, only that person can make him lose confidence. He is not swayed by gossip or rumors; he only watches action. Again, the difficult and best part about working with him are his high expectations. He undoubtedly demands a lot from the people he works with, but he also demands a lot of himself. Keith expects no less of you than what he expects of himself—and he sets the bar very high for himself.

With every achievement of his administration, the bar was raised. Mitchell had the same expectation of himself during negotiations at the highest levels globally.

Chapter Seven
A Healthy Lifestyle

Prime Minister Mitchell walks for Women's Health

It is safe to say that Keith Mitchell's youthful appearance is not maintained by genes alone, but by his attitude toward hard work and self-discipline. The people closest to him can attest to the fact that he is not easy to keep up with. He is up early physically exerting himself; running in the streets, along the beach or on a treadmill at the gym.

When Keith travels abroad, his ambassadors greeting him on arrival, could tell stories about trying to keep up with him as he crosses from the arrival gate at the airport, to waiting for transport. Everyone is breathless as he constantly moves. It's as if he is plugged into some energy source.

The Prime Minister never missed an opportunity to warn his closest officers, ambassadors and friends to do something about their physical health, reminding them that a healthy body is very important in a stressful job.

Looking at his practices, Keith Mitchell does not just go out preaching about fitness, he demonstrates this by vigorous living, being in good physical shape and adopting a healthy lifestyle. He gets down with the people to raise their spirits and build confidence. He takes his rest and his nutrition seriously as he measures his performance. He promotes social self-care and cultivates relationships with others. Old friends mean much to him. He always inquires and spares no chance to go to the boys to indulge in a game of dominos, drink some 'waters,' and he loves a good goat head soup and a fine glass of wine.

Looking at a game of US football is part of his recreation, as if to refresh his spirit and his comfort of belonging with the "boys." I remember him saying our country Grenada applauds the promotion of health through scientific and technological innovational concepts, as promoted in the US, China and other countries. Grenada support's the view, that the enhancement of people's health will be better achieved as a collective, with the help of institutional reforms and information sharing. That is why he strongly supports the position of the Caribbean Community and PAHO in their push to achieve the global embrace of the challenges we face with Non-Communicable Diseases (NCD), particularly in developing countries.

*Prime Minister Mitchell lectures at
American University Washington College of Law*

Whether a Member of Parliament as Prime Minister or Opposition Leader, he demonstrated respect for his station. In the years I worked with him, he was careful not to criticize a Grenadian public official simply to promote himself when representing his party abroad.

Still, he speaks candidly and is ready to meet the press and discuss pertinent issues about Grenada and the Caribbean. Transparency in governance is essential to confidence building, while being objective and forward looking. In 1995, soon after taking on the prime ministership for the first time, he established Grenada's first ever press secretariat. Within months he introduced weekly post Cabinet press briefings for members of the media.

PM Keith Mitchell with Ambassador
Dr. Denis G. Antoine at Grenada's
Independence Dinner.

Naturally a man of his people and for his people, self-aggrandizement is not his character. He is comfortable with the ordinary. Most notably, his office was never personalized. He stayed with tradition—maintaining the same decor as other governmental offices. For him, simple decor was a visual reminder of the importance of maintaining public trust.

Dr. Mitchell celebrates Grenadians for excelling in what they do, and reaches out to them wherever and whenever the opportunity is presented. It is no surprise that the Keith Mitchell Foundation centers on education. It was founded in January 2016 "To enhance the dignity and quality of life of needy individuals and families in Grenada, Carriacou and Petite Martinique." Specifically, aid is offered to students in their formative years who are pursuing an education to reach their full potential.

The Keith Mitchell that our people now know is a man whose dignity emanates from his modest family upbringing and his own path to knowledge, success and national leadership. His rise to national leadership was not happenstance. No task along the road to leadership was too small. A lesson he imparts on all of us is to show dignity in all that's done; but in the end, it depends on how well it's done and the conviction displayed in the application of oneself.

Someone who never met him, but watched him from afar in different situations, remarked, "Wow! That's a neighborhood brother." This neighborhood brother has grown to become the Nation's modern father figure. It is admirable how Dr. Mitchell keeps his head when he is maligned; and watch how he goes within himself and finds ways to deflect adversarial distractors with positive actions. Yes, he prays.

It is significant to note his catching sense of humor. This helps when dealing with detractors. He loves a good laugh and to become immersed in our folk culture and oral tradition. Keith is full of wit and self-expression that keeps him winning in life. At the heart of Keith Mitchell is a man who honors his friends and professional colleagues. Most importantly as a Dad he instills these values in his sentiments with his son Olinga.

When Dr. Mitchell speaks of friends, it is easy to tell by his tone. There is a calmness in his voice. Generally, Keith rarely shouts, apart from his well-modulated pitches in Parliament or when he is before the microphone in a public space.

One thing that must be understood about Dr. Mitchell, is his communication style. When in his presence, it is time to stop talking. When he gets silent and goes inward, and his lips go into a soliloquy, he leaves no hiding place for his disapproval. Even with his friends and close acquaintances, he tells it straight.

Chapter Eight
His People; an Extension of Himself

The man is comfortable in his skin, and he knows what time of the day it is. At ease with all groups and cultures, his global and social competence is astonishing. Keith certainly knows how to show appreciation to friends from near and far, and good friends are made to feel like family.

PM at Grenada Day in Brooklyn.

71

Dr. Mitchell has an amazing memory. He reminds us that we may not always recall what people do, but we always remember how they made us feel. He shows gratefulness to all—especially those who welcome his presence in their midst.

PM at Grenada Day in Brooklyn.

It is evident that Keith Mitchell takes pride in the image he casts as a representative for his country when traveling abroad. This fact is evidenced by the levity and appreciation he exhibits to those who support how he conducts his duties. There is willingness on the part of the US protective services to enable the least restrictive environment for him to maneuver.

PM Keith Mitchell, takes Prime Minister David Cameron of the United Kingdom on a public tour in Grenada.

Prime Minister Mitchell shares the occasion of the visit of Prime Minister Cameron of the UK, by taking him on a tour in Grenada. He points out areas in need of development that could use external support. Dr. Mitchell accords conscious respect to David Cameron because he interacts with reverence; for Cameron's recognition of the recoveries Grenada achieved following major natural disasters. One certainly got the impression that the relationship between David Cameron and

Keith Mitchell has been very positive.

It is appropriate and timely for Grenadians abroad and at home to reflect on and celebrate Dr. Keith Mitchell's leadership and his contributions to Grenada. He has accomplished significant milestones in his life; and has taken Grenada to a point in its history where global accolades are given as one of the top destinations in the world to visit. Because of Mitchell's enduring and effective leadership, Grenada is hailed as a model of good governance. Furthermore, under his leadership the lessons of Grenada are referenced for fiscal management and social mobility.

Keith Mitchell responds to the urges of his people when traveling abroad. His lively responses reflect this unique sense of placing value in the fact that anyone who comes to hear him or comes to express themselves in his presence, deserves respect for their attendance.

"They would not come if they did not care about something," Keith would say.

He often leans right into the crowd, pulls his acquaintances up, and reaches out to all well-wishers and spectators.

*Prime Minister leans into the crowd
of supporters in New York.*

A local family man, a native son, husband, father, now a mature statesman, has become the 'modern father' of our young nation. When celebrating Keith Mitchell, his dedication to Grenada and the Caribbean Community as a private citizen, regional public servant with global impact and his gifts to national and regional integration movements must be acclaimed.

His unassuming deportment and his genuine engagement with people reflect a man guided by the common values acquired from his humble beginnings. He entered public life with the same determination to succeed that he portrayed going into business or when it was his turn to perform during a cricket match. Simply put, he is an exceptionally hard worker, who plays to win in everything.

During his time in secondary school in Grenada, it is said that Mitchell was celebrated because of his close relations with classmates and the way he listened to them. He excelled in mathematics and athletics. Later, as a teacher, he went beyond the call of duty to help his pupils.

"My students reflect me," he once said. "Therefore, I want them to be the very best."

There is a phrase he tells anyone who needs to improve their work.

"You got to raise your game," he would say. This means, he expects more from you.

Chapter Nine
Cricket and Courage

The history of cricket in Grenada and the Caribbean records Mitchell's devotion as a friend of the game. While studying and working in the USA, he travelled in North America promoting and playing cricket. Through his passion for the game, he made many friends—that ultimately benefited Grenada.

But the value of friendship is more than having a personal relationship. For Keith Mitchell, and other national leaders that care about the prosperity of their   people, having friends means more support for the nation and the region.

Transferring his leadership skills to the field, as well as the discipline one needs to succeed in the game of cricket, he is wrapped in the passion and the conviction that his team will win, Mitchell interlocks with trusted friends as teammates for the public good.

Throughout the years, Keith maintained the desire to play competitively. He understands that the game remains a beloved tradition that defines Caribbean oneness. Therefore, as a leader, Keith Mitchell is competitive.

He seems well aware, like in the game of

cricket, forging trusted, reliable partnerships for the Caribbean Community is one of the strongest integrating forces for good.

***

Dr. Mitchell was effective as a leading negotiator and major contributor in the preparations for the Caribbean to host the 2007 ICC Cricket World Cup tournament. Mitchell still beams when he speaks of the fact that Grenada ably hosted first class games, along with the rest of the Caribbean.

Keith Mitchell's early entry into national politics occurred before leaving Grenada to study abroad and that prepared him well. His leadership skills were noticeable as a university student. He excelled in his chosen field of statistics and mathematics, and in sports. After graduating from UWI, he went on to complete graduate studies in the United States.

Driven by his passion to succeed, he became a college professor at the prestigious Howard University in Washington, D.C. His past students and professional colleagues refer to his tenure as being outstanding, particularly because he went out of his way to assist students and looked out for his colleagues as friends.

Following her visit to Grenada in 1994, and observing Dr. Mitchell in Grenada, Assistant

Professor of Medicine at Harvard University in Boston Dr. Cynthia Carter gave her reflection in a letter which said in part "……..This visit also had another positive result as I had the opportunity to meet one of my former professors at Howard University. I am talking about no lesser person than Dr. Keith Mitchell, who is now active in the local politics and who is a possible leader of your country……..."

As early as 1979, the opportunity to observe and work with Dr. Keith Mitchell became available to me. He was then a leading figure in the Grenadian and Caribbean Community in the Washington, D.C. area. He participated in strengthening national organizations such as Grenadians United, which were incredibly action oriented in diaspora matters and other activities focused on Grenada.

There is an honored Grenadian tradition that happens every Sunday that goes on (when weather permits) in the Washington, D.C. area. A close group of friends of a certain generation gather to play wind ball cricket. Mitchell was an active participant from the start. For over 40 years and counting whenever he visits Washington, D.C., Keith Mitchell asks about the boys in the park.

He promoted Grenadian and Caribbean interests abroad. He spoke up at a time when it was unpopular for Grenadians to speak up against many misguided activities that were occurring in Grenada. Through it all, he worked tirelessly. Keith Mitchell's roommates, while he worked and studied in Washington, D.C., recall that Mitchell consistently focused on the bigger picture, carried himself with respect and was respected by all people.

Generally, he sees work as a means-to-an-end, and that one's character is defined by how one works. The end must be borne in mind. He said whether it was on the switchboard as an attendant —in a large apartment building for students, in those days, keeping one's attention on the mission, was what counted for Keith Mitchell as he studied, and as he emerged as a leading professional in his field.

***

An undignified attempt to humiliate Keith Mitchell did not deter him. His good friend and dentist, recalled how Keith kept his composure when white neighbors surrounded his house with toilet paper upon moving into a neighborhood in Maryland. In those days, buying a home in that area was an act of bold integration. His presence alone as a black man was unwelcome. Keith knows how to keep his head when those around him are losing theirs.

80

He returned to Grenada during the time of governmental crisis and a period of unpredictable transition in 1983. The country was wrestling with the transition to democratic governance as a means of recovery from the plunge it took into communism.

Just before returning to Grenada to enter national politics as a candidate for election, when asked about taking leadership, Mitchell emphasized that leadership was not a priority for him at that time. Looking at Mitchell's administrative career, following his return to Grenada provides a most interesting profile of guts and skills.

***

The coming together of the New National Party, (NNP), led by the late Herbert Blaize, gave hope—considering the doctrinal chaos that existed in Grenada. The eyes of the US and the global community were on Grenada, following the ill-fated revolution led by the late Maurice Bishop.

"Because of the fragile situation in our country, I am going back because I am optimistic," said Mitchell. True to his character, Keith Mitchell remained in touch with the small group of active supporters in Washington D.C., New York, and Canada. He has always avowed that North American support with good friends is important to

81

the interest of Grenada. Strategically, Mitchell leveraged support offered by the Institute for Republicans International.

"The strengthening and building of the infrastructure of our democratic institutions is necessary," Mitchell explained. The NNP was registered as a member of the International Democratic Union (IDU) and was positioned as a Centrist Right Party. The NNP with support of the IDU, was entrusted with stabilizing the situation in Grenada.

Mitchell remained firm in his commitment to take advantage of training opportunities for citizens entering public service. At that time in Grenada, many highly skilled and educated Grenadians had emigrated. The population dipped, and it became obvious that the road to recovery and democratic governance presented major challenges. The task embraced by Keith Mitchell broadened. He regularly returned to Washington, D.C. seeking support, and to give updates to Grenadians about the situation at home.

At the end of the interim government, a mandated general election was held in December 1984. Keith Mitchell was elected to represent the constituency of Saint George North West in the House of Representatives. Too this day he has held the seat in every subsequent election. What is even more significant is the fact that as a Member of

-1-

Political Leader's Message

This convention is indeed an historic one for our 10 year old party for three reasons -
1. It is the first convention being held with General Elections just a few months away.
2. It is being held in the presence of scores of our Caribbean friends from the (a) Eastern Caribbean Institute for Democracy (ECID) and (b) both the Youth and Women's Arm of ECID.
3. It is being held in an atmosphere of the most severe economic pressures ever experienced by all our people.
With the above in mind I wish to impress on all our party members the tremendous responsibilities we face in ensuring that the NNP forms the next government with a convincing majority. The momentum and spirit of the convention must be carried throughout Grenada, Carriacou and Petit Martinique. Our main task in winning must be to cure the economic, political and social ills. by rekindling the now dormant national spirit.
On behalf of our party, I wish to express sincere thanks to our Caribbean Brothers and Sisters for their presence at a most crucial time for our country.
To all our Delegates, Observers, Invited Guests, the Press - I thank you all.

MAY GOD BLESS EACH AND EVERYONE.

Parliament (MP) he remains   effective and demonstrates great competence on the floor of the Lower House in the same manner he accounts and performs his ministerial duties.

To this day, he remains focused on the needs of the people who elected him. He attends to their concerns, and he listens and pays attention to their livelihood. I have observed the way he places high priority on the impact of his work abroad and the needs of Grenada. He paid attention then, and now he puts the needs of Grenadians and their families above all else.

It is easy to recall his personal support for the education of the children of individuals who worked in his home. A remarkable example is when he sponsored the cost for a child to go abroad to study at his alma mater, Howard University; because he said, "That's a bright girl and she will go very far."   These personal actions are taken discreetly and transcend the call of duty, yet remain a quiet practice that should not go unnoticed.

Keith Mitchell shows courage by the way he conducts himself. It's said that in difficult and challenging times, courageous men step up. And when there is no courage, out of courage, brave men come forward.   Frankly speaking, Keith Mitchell, bravely stands up when thousands of 'faux' prime ministers eagerly criticize everything.

84

Despite this, Keith allows them to speak freely, as he remains focused as the leader of all.

Chapter Ten
Strategic Leadership

Hon. Keith C. Mitchell shouldered the leadership of the NNP over thirty years ago; at times when there were competitive relationships inside the relatively new party—in existence for just about five years. The demand for effective leadership became contentious with four potential leaders in the party: Hon. Herbert Blaize, Hon. George Brizan, Dr. Hon. Francis Alexis, with all eyes on Hon. Keith Mitchell.

It was a time when courage was needed to stand up to Herbert Blaize. Nonetheless, it was difficult when other aspiring leaders began to push against Keith, leveraging for their turn at the helm.

He soon realized that how he executed his duties as an MP gave him much needed skills for future leadership by sharpening his effective management dexterities.

Mitchell bravely stepped up when it counted at the NNP convention to openly present his readiness to lead the NNP and raise the profile of the party. As a result, the rank and file elected Keith Claudius Mitchell as leader of the New National Party, defeating Prime Minister Herbert Blaize at the open convention.

To become the leading man did not sit well with the elder Blaize. It came as no surprise to many that on July 12, 1989, Keith Mitchell, who was then very visible in the eyes of the nation, was dismissed from his ministerial position by Mr. Blaize. It was a ministry that Mitchell managed well —the Minister of Works and Communications. And he also served as Minister of Communications, Works and Public Utilities, Cooperatives, Community Development, Women's Affairs and Civil Aviation from 1988 to 1998.

*A light hearted moment Amb Antoine pinning
PM at emulation ceremony.*

The NNP lost the national election in 1990, then was victorious in the general election on June 20, 1995, winning eight out of 15 seats in the House of Representatives.

Dr. Keith C. Mitchell took office as Prime Minister of Grenada, for the first time along with his Cabinet, on June 22, 1995. Under his leadership, the party won all 15 seats in an early election in January 1999.

In the November 2003 election the NNP narrowly won a third term to remain in power with a one-seat parliamentary majority.

Notwithstanding the sustainable efforts of the New National Party, it was defeated in the general election held on July 8, 2008 by the National Democratic Congress (NDC). The NNP won four seats against 11 for the NDC. Mitchell retained his seat. The NDC leader, Mr. Tillman Thomas succeeded Mitchell as Prime Minister on July 9, 2008. Mitchell said that the people voted for change and congratulated Thomas. Following the election, he continued as NNP leader and was sworn in as Leader of the Opposition on July 16, 2008.

Mitchell was never daunted while in opposition. He simply raised his game as MP and party leader. In the February 2013 general election, the NNP won all 15 parliamentary seats. After this resounding victory, Mitchell was sworn in as Prime Minister on February 20, 2013. Looking ahead to the next election, Mitchell predicted that his party could win all 15 seats in Parliament for a third time. Dr. Mitchell and the NNP created history by retaining all 15 seats in the Grenada General Election on March 13, 2018. It is the first time any political party under the same leadership, regionally or otherwise, achieved such a feat.

It is worth repeating that since Dr. Keith Mitchell was first elected, he has been serving Grenada gallantly; as a parliamentarian and political leader. Today, he is one of the longest serving statesmen, Member of Parliament and Head of Government in the Caribbean. Most notably, he is the longest serving Prime Minister of Grenada.

Dr. Keith Mitchell has a track record of success in private and public life. I consider him an excellent role model of what one can achieve through hard work and dedication. Serving as Prime Minister of Grenada, Dr. the Rt. Hon. Keith C. Mitchell demonstrated effective leadership and vision in his quest to move Grenada forward. That he remained preoccupied with finding opportunities for young Grenadians is perhaps one of his most driving ardors. His strong stance on better education and training for the empowerment of youth in Grenada, and more importantly, the action taken by his administration, positioned the Grenada Youth Enterprise Initiative as a regional stand-out model.

Chapter Eleven
Establishing Friendship for
National Good

The courageous guidance of Prime Minister
Mitchell carried Grenada through the
unprecedented periods of recovery from natural
disasters, which brought death and devastation after
the wrath of Hurricanes Ivan and Emily in 2004
and 2005, respectively. In addition, the Prime
Minister has managed the affairs of Government
through perilous recuperation periods from serious
economic downturns,   brought about by the
imprudent management of previous
administrations.

The Prime Minister places confidence and
has shown appreciation by his thoughtful
introduction of several foreign nationals as persons
of trust after intense scrutiny. Afterwards, they were
seen as partners in the development of Grenada.
These individuals must have the best interest of
Grenada in mind, with good intentions to
contribute to the prosperity of the nation. They
must be engaged in positive promotion and
advancement of the country for the benefit of all
citizens. Mitchell has accommodated the inclusion
of foreign nationals that serve with distinction and

make sacrifices beyond expectation. Many have remained faithful doing so—even the ultimate sacrifice of death has occurred.

Keith Mitchell has not failed to return his gratitude to such persons. He has conferred the rights and privileges of citizenship to worthy individuals, only after exhaustive clearance for good character. It is noteworthy that the friends of Grenada do not serve Keith Mitchell. Instead, they are resources for the greater good working with different executives; this, despite criticism when the opposing party is out of office.

Dr. Mitchell always reminds Grenadians that several foreign nationals made friendly contributions to help Grenada. Among these friends of Grenada, is 'Bart' Lawson. Bart was a philanthropist introduced to Grenada by the late Ambassador Stanislaus, who made it a point to highlight Bart's invaluable contribution to Grenada. Sadly, Bart Lawson died while visiting Grenada in order to erect children's playgrounds at various locations. In gratefulness, the Prime Minister continues to express his gratitude to the son of 'Bart' who was a toddler when his father died many years ago.

The Prime Minister listens and converses with people who have shown interest in doing business in Grenada. He shares the values and culture of our country with those who have taken the time to engage in promoting Grenada's investment climate. The Prime Minister serves as Grenada's number one marketing agent for investment projects in Grenada.

When traveling abroad he seeks agreements with educational institutions in search of scholarships. He has a desire to find every opportunity to place young Grenadians in universities and colleges. He never hesitated to sit down and negotiate scholarships with presidents, provosts and other academic leaders.

What many Grenadians may not know is how driven Keith Mitchell has been from the start, and still moved to find innovative ways to assist Grenadian students with meeting the cost of their tuition.

A very innovative and brilliant initiative was undertaken by the Embassy in Washington, D.C. urging to assist in the promotion of a commemorative Grenada stamp collection. That collection of stamps, in the US philatelic market featured the life of the late Ronald Regan, former President of the USA.

Prime Minister Keith Mitchell chats with
First Lady Nancy Reagan at the ranch in California.

Through this initiative, under the auspices of the Embassy of Grenada in Washington, D.C, the Prime Minister launched the Ronald Regan Scholarship Fund. All proceeds from the sale of that stamp finance a scholarship program to assist Grenadian students by helping to meet financial shortfalls and enable them to remain in their program of studies until graduation.

The successful sale of stamps provides financial assistance for young Grenadians who were studying abroad, including within **CARICOM**, wherever they were sent on government scholarship. This initiative serves two important purposes: helps meet government obligations, and aids students who encounter financial hardships.

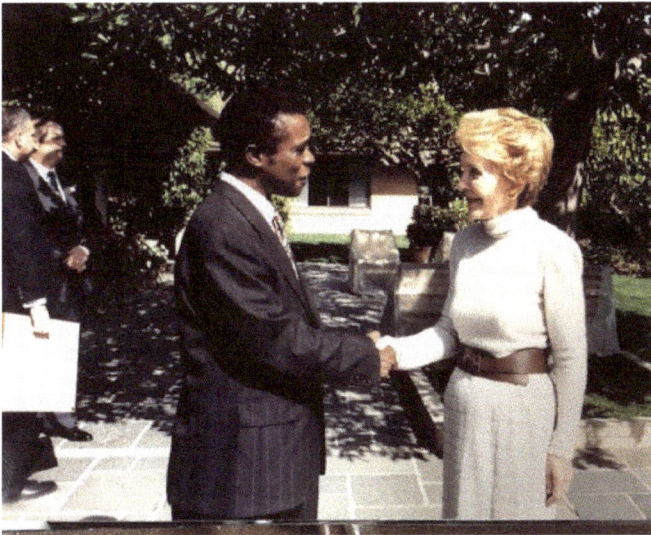

PM welcomed by Nancy Reagan to the
Regan Ranch bringing stamps for scholarship.

His vision was to enable these students to meet the heavy burden of financing their studies. I recall the Prime Minister making a trip to the Regan Ranch in California to hand deliver a set of stamps, and requesting Nancy Regan to have the

Regan Library register the stamps in support of the scholarship fund.

I travelled with Keith to Tallahassee Florida, where he received an honorary degree and pushed for scholarship and training for young Grenadians. It was such a grueling journey because there were many stops and transfers, but he said we must go because the children need opportunities.

In New York, there are friends beyond the Grenada diaspora; there are friends that stand up when the Prime Minister calls; they have demonstrated commitment to a win-win engagement with Grenada.

Chapter Twelve
Building Resiliency to Climate Change

I recall sitting at the Embassy of Grenada in Washington, D.C. in the immediate wake of the hurricanes that knocked Grenada down. There was no knowledge of the scope of the disaster, except having to respond to parents and loved ones about the status of their families in Grenada. Added to that, were the frantic calls from family and friends of students at St. George's University.

There was no one to turn to because communication broke down. The home of the Prime Minister was destroyed and the island was cut off from the world. However, Keith Mitchell was one of the first persons reached by the Embassy. He took refuge on a boat in the St. George's harbor, where he used the facilities of the British to reach out for help from the international community— and to make contact with his diplomatic representatives and friends abroad.

At a meeting with Caribbean delegations and international community partners during a World Bank Group—IMF Annual Meeting, one of his main messages was focused on preparedness for natural disasters. Specifically, to build more resilience, and plan for a more sustainable future.

Grenada's Prime Minister Mitchell pledged then, that Grenada remains determined to build back better after Hurricane Ivan in 2004.

"In this crisis, let's not miss the opportunity for change, we have no time to waste," Mitchell said.

In the days and months following the hurricane disasters, Grenada was fortunate to have such a leader. The international community recognized the caliber of the man. Keith Mitchell engaged the World Bank and the donor community in Washington, D.C. where he eloquently presented Grenada's case for support to the satisfaction of all partners.

His brilliance and well-prepared accounting of the situation in Grenada, resulted in the establishment of a precedent setting initiative called the Agency for Reconstruction and Development (ARD), with the mandate to build back better. Under the watchful eyes of the Prime Minister, tremendous strides were made. From my observation, among the many benefits from this Agency were innovative social recovery programs, a human settlement policy, strategic land use, building codes and better planning. Projects undertaken by the ARD spanned several sectors, from a Construction Quality Assurance Mechanism with a Model Home Construction Repair Contract for house holders and contractors to a draft National

Strategic Development Plan. The ARD established several data bases during its three-year tenure. The leadership and staff of the agency deserve full accolades.

The revitalization of the agricultural sector, infrastructure, tourism, private enterprise and above all, attention paid to education, sports and health care, had a tremendously historic and positive impact on the nation. Keith Mitchell's efforts then continue to shape Grenada now. As further demonstration of his character and leadership, it's only fitting to say that his will to build Grenada was as strong as 'Stone'—a nickname he was given. I say strong as ironstone, indeed.

Among the proudest moments for me, being in the presence of Keith Mitchell, was the occasion of his speech during the historic Conference on the Caribbean, convened in Washington, D.C., with the President of the United States, and other Caribbean Heads of State and Government on June 19 – 21, 2007.

Dr. the Honorable Keith Mitchell made the following intervention:

It was here in Washington, D.C. in 2002 that the concept of a multidimensional approach to security was conceptualized. The countries of the Caribbean, without exception, are all developing states, and in most cases, Small

101

Island developing states, which are challenged by the peculiar vulnerabilities occasioned by size.

We have resolutely stood with the international community in the global fight against terrorism and have played active roles in the ongoing process of codifying regimes to consolidate international peace and security. But while the vagaries of terrorism and the avoidance of a modern nuclear arms race are important global issues, the exceptional circumstances of small size and vulnerability make the maintenance of environmental security as vital to our nations as any other threat to global security.

While the fight to preserve our environmental security is a global one, the effects are not quit so. The cruel irony of the environmental issued like climate change is that it is the smallest and most vulnerable who have contributed the least to the problem that will be hardest hit. For us in the Caribbean, security extends well beyond the notion of traditional border security and territorial integrity; it is an all-encompassing concept which requires us to treat holistically with the key development issues, including environmental security, which are critical to our developmental aspirations.

Today, our national are still grappling with the mitigation of the effects of climate change and consequential sea level rise. While we have made important advances through the establishment of the Caribbean Climate Change Center, adaption while critical, is simply not enough. While we debate, it is estimated that the concentration of carbon in the earth's atmosphere has risen to 380 Parts per Million (PPM) in 2006, from 280 Parts per Million (PPM) in the pre–industrial era. When the other greenhouse gases are added that total rises to 425 PPM's. That has given rise to an increase in temperature of 1.35 degrees Fahrenheit.

This is an increase that has never been seen in the course of history. In the face of the resounding evidence not only of the impact, but the anticipated damage to humankind and our natural environment, any further debate on whether climate change is real or imagined is anathema to any aspirations of a future for generations to come.

Still, important strides have been made at a global level to arrest environmental degradation and I am pleased that the Caribbean region has been at the vanguard of efforts to protect the global environment. We therefore welcome the G8 decision to conduct the climate change negotiations within the framework of the United Nations. But much work remains to be done and the window of opportunity for us to make a real impact is small.

There is a need for deep and rapid reductions of greenhouse gas emissions by major emitters within the next 10 – 15 years in keeping with the principle of common but differentiated responsibilities and respective capacities. In the area of environmental management, we must continue to work together as a global community to set broad policy objectives and standards which are then implemented through national and regional initiatives.

Concerted action within a multilateral framework must be complemented by concrete initiatives emerging from regional and bilateral for a, such as the one in which we are presently engages this afternoon. The international community is converging around a target for greenhouse gas (GHG) emissions at a level that would stabilize the resulting temperature increases at 2 Degrees Celsius (2ºC), above pre-industrial levels. Long-term temperature increase however, will have to be stabilized well below 2 Degrees Celsius in order to sustain the viability of island nations.

In fact, at temperatures higher than 2 Degrees Celsius, there will be irreparable damage to coral reefs, declines in food crops, stronger tropical storms and cyclones, decreased water availability and increased melting of the Greenland ice sheets with long term implications for sea level rise.

Here again brothers and sisters, while there is a multilateral framework for addressing these issues, the Caribbean and the United States have justifiable cause for bilateral cooperation based on the unique challenges faced by our neighboring countries. Global standards establish important benchmarks for the international community, but we must undertake among ourselves to go beyond the minimum standards established globally ad take concrete steps to effectively tackle this "sleeping dragon."

Our countries have separately taken to negotiating "WTO–plus" trading agreements, so too we must apply a higher threshold for our environmental policy.

My dear brothers and sisters, technology has an important role to play in bridging the gap between environmental sustainability and economic growth. Resource productivity in the global economy is being revolutionized by technology. Since the industrial revolution, economic growth and energy growth have been interwoven in a cycle of codependence. Technology is changing that, but the Caribbean requires the assistance of our more developed neighbors in accessing new technologies and the financing to implement the requisite modernization of our productive processes.

While we welcome the advances made by entrepreneurs in the region to harness solar energy, and the new initiatives which will look at utilizing wind and wave energies, these initiatives require technical assistance and investment in research and development.

These areas as well as capacity building are important elements of a possible deepened partnership. Indeed, if we in the Americas and specifically the Caribbean and the United States are serious about alleviating poverty, improving access to health and health care as well as maintaining peace and security, environment security will be vital to our developmental goals.

Projections at the turn of the new millennium estimated that the new targets set by the Millennium Development Goals (MDG's) and reinforced by the Monterrey consensus of 2002, would see Overseas Development Assistance (ODA) reach an estimated $88 billion by 2010. The true picture is that the actual levels of ODA have fallen far below expectations. ODA t the region has been in steady decline over the years. I think we are all aware of this.

The region has done well over the years to achieve a level of development that belies its inherent vulnerability to external shocks. Certainly, my own country understands how years of progress and development can be obliterated by a single natural disaster. Just to remind you that in just over an hour, we lost over 200 % of GDP and you don't recover overnight. The need for support continues.

Colleagues, it should be clear that our environmental security cannot be extricated from our overall security in the region. It is inextricably woven into the continued viability and development objectives. Having agreed to this in multiple global arenas as demonstrated by our signature of nearly every multilateral agreement on environment policy, the onus now rests with us to devise concrete steps to make the best use of our bilateral relations to give effect to the policy initiatives we have undertaken.

There is a strong case to be made also for small

states like those in the Caribbean to receive priority in the provision of funding and technical assistance. Limited technical capacity at the national level compromises our ability to always take advantage of available mechanisms effectively.

Colleagues, the challenge for us today as we discuss environmental security is to chart for ourselves an escape from the dead-end paths that have unfortunately characterized many of these environmental debates globally. We don't really have a choice you know, to make between environmental and economic development. Instead, these two concepts must go hand in hand and are indeed key components in our approach to continue security and stability in the region.

They form fertile ground for partnership and the development of strong and viable legacies upon which our growth and development are hinged. When our children judge the advances of our generation, my dear brothers and sisters let it be that we have left a legacy of growth, high aspirations and exponential growth that has not compromised the promise of a bright future for generations to come.

We must befriend rich and poor nations alike, small and vast, and certainly among neighbors, act responsibly, collaboratively, and with foresight which guarantees the hope of a bright future.

I sincerely hope that at the end of these meetings that we all leave this city declaring that we have agreed to bold innovative steps to address the serious environmental issues which challenge us, and the means of financing them. Thank You.

Chapter Thirteen
Presence in the International Community

Pride in country at a time in our history when everyone writes their own history, requires that we reach a national consensus that Keith Mitchell is accorded recognition by all Grenadians in the same manner as CARICOM citizens and global leaders. Give credit to Keith Mitchell for placing Grenada on the highest level of Island States.

More Grenadians should proudly join members of the global community in expressing admiration for the economic achievements of our country and its comeback under his leadership. Grenada is globally respected as a prominent example for other small nation states. It is clear that Keith Mitchell is in the prime of his professional competence as a public servant and party leader.

***

When asked—Grenadians and particularly, non-citizens, what they like about the Rt. Hon. Keith Mitchell, some of the following responses were given:

"A great leader. A person that cares and loves his nation and its people and wants the best for them."

"What I like about Keith Mitchell is that he masters or understands the culture and mindset of the people he leads, and uses it to the advantage of the country."

"He's patient and is strategic in dealing with opposition or distracters. He is very loyal to those he believes are loyal to him. He doesn't like pretentious people, but he finds ways to deal with them."

"He is a master politician, determined and confident. He has achieved greatness despite coming from humble beginnings. He is an example to everyone including the less fortunate, of what can be achieved in life."

"I have known him since the days of the Advisory Council of Grenada when he was a member. During those years I have seen him grow into a very savvy politician and leader. To me, he seems to be committed to the good of his country and does what he can to advance Grenada on the world stage, while improving the lives of Grenadians."

"He is approachable, can be "down to earth" when the situation warrants, and can be "up on top" when the situation arises. In other words, he can rub shoulders with the common man, as well as those in high circles. Last, but not least, he has a sense of humor, and he is very intelligent."

***

I have personally seen that Dr. Mitchell has not allowed his profession, nor his office, to become his identity. That's what makes him a great leader. He continues to make history. His legacy will center on his impact on our country's development. We will remember the substantial improvements to the quality of life brought about by his administrations. Keith Mitchell's leadership, his ministerial portfolios, and management style, have brought about the greatest measure of social mobility Grenada has seen.

Dr. Mitchell's rise to national leadership did not come by a sudden jump. His résumé of professional success and contributions outside politics bear evidence of his toils. It is etched in our modern history that the social transformation brought about in Grenada since 1974 was shaped by the roles played by Keith Mitchell. In short, he has continuously made a tremendously positive impact on Grenada as we know it today.

It is my privilege to salute the Rt. Hon. Keith Mitchell, as he keeps Grenada moving from strength to strength. May God continue to bless him, his family, the NNP and the people of Grenada.

This sentiment flows as supporters of the party and country gather to take full advantage of Keith's presence   when the opportunity arises to converse with him. The gatherings usually take place in welcoming environments with Grenadians in Brooklyn New York. Prime Minister Mitchell blends in with the most passionate contributors— the ones most concerned about the social and cultural development of Grenada. Keith encourages Grenadians abroad to remain engaged in philanthropic and direct technical support in education, healthcare and in various parishes and villages throughout Grenada.

***

Dr. Mitchell prioritizes finding ways to express appreciation for the sustained efforts of Grenadians who achieve high levels of success. This acknowledgment encourages them to give back to their local communities and become vested in national efforts. Overall, Keith is never stingy about showing his genuine love. He exudes joy when among his people, when traveling in New York, Toronto, London and around the world. He relentlessly encourages those with requisite skills to present themselves to fill positions and invest in the country.

Chapter Fourteen
Historic Political Record

In November 2017 there was a discussion about the record terms of appointment of Keith Mitchell as Prime Minister of Grenada, and the scope of his work for Grenada. My good friend, Dr. Spencer, said to me then that Dr. Mitchell will be moved only by God, and the people, that's how he sees it. Dr. Linus Spencer Thomas was right when he called to say, "Man, clean sweep again, and my prediction was on target."

And sure enough on February 13, 2018, another chapter in the history of political leadership was written in Grenada. On Election Day, it was the dawn of a new era. It is appropriate to recall that on March 13, 1979, Grenadians were arrested with fear during a violent coup d'état, when the rein of Government was seized by guns. In glaring contrast on March 13, 2018, 39 years later, the Government of Grenada, under the leadership of Keith Claudius Mitchell, provided an environment for Grenadians to go to the poles in a free and fair national election. Grenadians voted in a celebratory fashion, singing and dancing, and free from fear to express themselves.

113

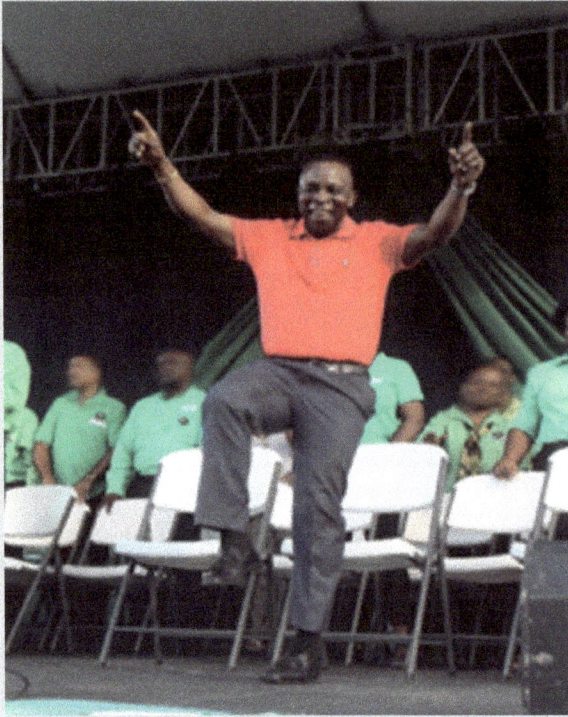

*PM doing the unforgettable
victory dance.*

Without fear that anyone would die, citizens lined up and voted. In a jubilant manner, they engraved into history for an unprecedented third time, their admiration and confidence in the leadership of Keith Claudius Mitchell and the New National Party. The significance of this historic event is the commemorative nature of the moment.

114

Once again, in a magnanimous way, Keith C. Mitchell, humbly accepted victory and recognized that the opposition had to be congratulated. He recognized the opposition also had the support of citizens who must benefit from a government called to represent everyone. But what a memorable victory dance he gave the nation.

Keith Claudius Mitchell is one of the most significant people I met while studying and working in the United States of America. What's more, working with him for the betterment of Grenada for the past thirty years of my life has undoubtedly been a continuous learning experience. In 1980, I was intrigued and wanted to know more about Keith C. Mitchell. However, my association with Dr. Keith C. Mitchell began years before, when we met on the campus of Howard University. I attended a summer class, and remember that even then, Keith was passionately absorbed in all things about Grenada, and trying to garner attention for the island nation from all who would listen.

As a professor of Mathematics at Howard University, he was well respected among his peers, his students and staff. But he was more than a professor. The Keith Mitchell I met then was a tutor, a Caribbean community activist; already a leader. He functioned as a resource to anyone who reached out to him. He quietly led and interacted with the Caribbean community. In sports, he brought the Caribbean together by raising the profile of cricket in the United States. Mitchell engaged not only Grenadians, but effectively rallied all CARICOM nationals and encouraged them to connect. He had global reach within the Caribbean and commonwealth communities.

He remained driven, moved by demonstrating entrepreneurship skills and industriousness, working his way through school. Mitchell brought dignity to whatever job he took. The man I know as Keith Mitchell remains inspired by excellence, continuous growth and the success that follows. Applying his brilliance in math and statistics, he provided services in tax preparation, tutoring for his peers, students and anyone who needed help with computation. He enjoyed those activities, which seemed to come very easily to him —a gift.

Keith C. Mitchell influenced many in his time abroad. It was his influence that encouraged me to join his group, focused on increasing awareness regarding the unfortunate drift occurring in the very early period of the ill-fated Revolution.

Dr. Mitchell's record as a scientist and his leadership in the Caribbean Community on matters of science and technology helped position Grenada as a leading voice relating to the application of

116

science and technology in solving the climate crisis. A new CARICOM Quasi Cabinet portfolio for Science and Technology, including Information and Communications, was created under his leadership.

Indeed, his leadership helped to increase Grenada's engagement in global climate change and renewable energy consensus building. Now, Grenada's contributions are highly acclaimed.

In the fight for protective action and policy adjustments to combat the negative impacts of climate change, he emerged as one of the most determined Caribbean and Small Island Developing States (SIDS) leaders to push for climate resilience practices. In many ways, he was emboldened by the Hurricane Ivan experience that happened under his watch. Mitchell was emphatic about positioning Grenada as a global model. He did not want the trauma of Ivan to occur again. As a result of his work, Mitchell's voice is well respected in the climate change discourse regionally and globally.

Proponents of the Green Climate Fund (GCF), note his direct appeal for decisive action towards transformational adaptation and mitigation measures to save and protect SIDS on the planet.

Mitchell calls on his regional colleagues and world leaders to take note of the increasingly visible and devastating impacts of climate change. He often cautions that the impacts will continue, and never squanders an opportunity to plead for

117

collective action. He understands well that there are the common risks of climate change, therefore we should create corridors to critical modification and relief action.

Reference is made to the Intergovernmental Panel on Climate Change (IPCC) Special Report on Global Warming of 1.5 degrees Celsius. Dr. Mitchell said, "It presented convincing, indisputable scientific evidence of the impact of human induced activities on global warming."

The IPCC report also addressed the potential impact on human survival. Dr. Mitchell noted that it cannot be business as usual.

"Future generations will applaud us for the actions we ought to take now to preserve the planet. The threat of climate change is real, it is here and we have a short window to avert catastrophic disasters of unimaginable proportions," the Prime Minister stated.

As a staunch supporter of climate change adaptation measures, Dr. Mitchell highlighted the need for a regional re-commitment to champion the full replenishment of the GCF.

"The need for support from the donor countries in this process cannot be over-emphasized," he said. And added that Grenada and its Caribbean sisters and brothers will stand shoulder to shoulder with the GCF, in advocating the need for donor support.

He expressed support for the thrust to ensure that adequate, predictable and grant-based climate change financing is directly accessible to the most vulnerable island states.

"I champion the call to look beyond the per capita Gross Domestic Product (GDP) of our countries, as the yardstick to determine eligibility for concessionary climate financing. The special circumstances and unique vulnerabilities of Small Island Developing States do not evaporate with graduation through per capita income classification schemes," he said.

He readily responds to visit UWI. When invited, mention is made of his growing influence on national and regional fronts. Moreover, his leadership must be observed by his service to his people on the ground in his community— particularly in his constituency. What is most impressive are his 'clinical political skills'. He leads by giving attention to the needs of his people, he attends to them one by one, listening and responding respectfully and privately. As a political practitioner, Dr. Mitchell's conduct of allowing himself to be led by his constant search for solutions, in order to meet the needs of his country, is an unmatched healthy political practice.

119

Chapter Fifteen
Return to Cave Hill

At the third Prime Minister's Lecture held at The University of the West Indies (UWI), in his capacity as Prime Minister, addressed the student body group, 'UWI Students Today Alumni Tomorrow' also known as STAT. His address, *The Use of Technology in Unlocking Caribbean Potential in Order to Create Further Development*, centered on how Caribbean students can shape the world with technological pursuits.

Dr. Wendy C. Grenade, a Grenadian and lecturer in Political Science at The UWI Cave Hill Campus, made the following observations about Keith Mitchell when she introduced then Prime Minister Mitchell on 10 April, 2013. In her introduction, Dr. Grenade presented some facts about the achievements and the character of Keith Mitchell to the faculty and students as he returned to the same campus where he studied. These were her remarks:

Ladies and gentlemen, students, it is my pleasure to introduce to you this evening, Dr. the Right Honourable Keith Claudius Mitchell, Prime Minister of Grenada, Carriacou and Petit Martinique, to deliver the third Prime Ministerial lecture—organized by UWI Students Today Alumni Tomorrow. This evening's lecture, on the theme: "The Use of Technology in Unlocking Caribbean Potential in order to create further Development" is an opportunity to draw from Dr. Mitchell's profound insights on issues critical to Caribbean development.

Dr. Keith Mitchell holds a Bachelor of Science Degree in Mathematics and Chemistry from our own University of the West Indies, a master's degree from Howard University, and a Doctorate in Mathematics and Statistics from the American University. He is a veteran politician, an astute leader, who skillfully bridges generational and class divides. A friend of the business class; yet a champion of the poor and dispossessed. We often refer to Grenada as a small country with a big history. For almost thirty years, Keith Claudius Mitchell, contributed in extraordinary ways to the Grenadian polity, economy, and society.

In 1983, Dr. Keith Mitchell left Washington, DC, where he was a tenured Professor of Mathematics at Howard University, to contribute to Grenada's rebuilding process. In the 1984 elections, Dr. Mitchell was elected Member of Parliament for St. George Northwest, and he has successfully contested that seat in every subsequent election. During his early political career, Dr. Mitchell's portfolio included responsibility for the Ministry of Communications, Works, and Public Utilities. Even his detractors will agree that he transformed Grenada's infrastructural landscape. Many rural communities received electricity, water, telephone, and paved roads for the first time, under his watch.

Dr. Mitchell was elected Political Leader of the New National Party (NNP) in 1989 and successfully led that party to victory in 1995, 1999, 2003 and recently in February this year. History will record that the NNP, under Dr. Mitchell's leadership, is the only political party in the Caribbean that made a clean sweep of the polls; winning every single parliamentary seat in two general elections; 1999 and 2013.

Dr. Mitchell is a skilled coach and team leader. His political skill cannot be delinked from his attachment to sport and to cricket. Dr. Mitchell was a member of the Grenada Cricket Team from 1964 to 1966. In 1973 he was made Captain of the Grenada Cricket Team as well as the combined Windward and Leeward Youth Cricket Team.

An avid cricketer, he has mastered the art of bowling his opponents clean and sweeping electoral test matches and even series. Today, as many political parties are undergoing leadership crises, Dr. Mitchell must be commended for his political skill and leadership of the New National Party.

Beyond the party, Dr. Mitchell has demonstrated decisive leadership in Government. For example, after Hurricane Ivan severely devastated Grenada in 2004, under the leadership of Prime Minister Keith Mitchell, and with tremendous assistance from our OECS and CARICOM neighbors, and the international community, Grenada embarked on a most successful recovery.

Women's participation in party politics is one of Grenada's long traditions. During Prime Minister Mitchell's reign, from 1995 to 2008, several women held key positions in the Cabinet and other branches of government.

Only last evening, in a national address, Prime Minister Mitchell announced that Grenada's next Head of State will be a woman, Dr. Cecile La Grenade, a prominent and successful Grenadian businesswoman. This announcement was made even as Grenadians are still paying tribute to the late Dame Hilda Bynoe, who was the first native governor of Grenada, from 1967 to 1972. In fact she was the first female governor in the British Commonwealth. Dame Hilda Bynoe passed away in Trinidad earlier this week.

Prime Minister Mitchell's impact transcends the Grenadian political landscape. He is a nationalist and regionalist. It was at Cave Hill, I am sure, that the seeds of regionalism were sworn in Prime Minister Mitchell's spirit. His Barbadian wife is testament to this.

In his capacity as Prime Minister, Dr. Mitchell has served on two occasions as Chairman of the Caribbean Community. He has also served as Chairman of the Board of Governors of the Caribbean Development Bank; the Ministerial Council of the Association of Caribbean States; the OECS and the longest-serving chairman of the Regional Security System. Prime Minister Mitchell was also instrumental in leading a regional team to resolve internal disputes in Guyana.

Importantly, he was Chairman of CARICOM's sub-committee on Cricket and showed regional leadership at some of the most tenuous moments of West Indies Cricket. In CARICOM, Grenada has lead responsibility for Science and

Technology and that country has spearheaded the Caribbean Knowledge and Learning Network. Dr. Mitchell is, therefore, well placed to address us on the theme "The Use of Technology in Unlocking Caribbean Potential in order to create further Development."

This is a most relevant topic for the current Caribbean moment. This year, we celebrate 40 years since the signing of the Treaty of Chaguaramas that established CARICOM.

We are also celebrating 50 years since the Cave Hill Campus of the University of the West Indies was established. These regional institutions reflect our collective gains, through common struggle. At a time when Caribbean countries, individually and collectively, are continuing to search for new pathways to development, science and technology must be a critical cornerstone of economic transformation going forward.

Ladies and gentlemen, students, on November 12, 1946 the late Dowlyn and still vibrant Catherine Mitchell gave to Grenada and the Caribbean an extraordinary son. The constituents of St. George North West have given to Grenada a veteran politician. The Cave Hill Campus of the UWI has given to the Caribbean and indeed the world a regionalist, who has served and will continue to serve Grenada and the Caribbean region with distinction.

Welcome home, Dr. Mitchell. As a member of the Grenada Association of Barbados and a Grenadian who lectures at the University of the West Indies, Cave Hill Campus, I am proud to welcome you to address us on this most important topic: "The Use of Technology in Unlocking

Caribbean Potential to create further Development."
Welcome!"

It is worth noting that after Cave Hill, the
Prime Minister's biography, reflected below, is his
continuing education and accomplishment profile.
The PM worked as a professional consultant to
many government departments and private
corporations in the United States.

Keith Claudius Mitchell received his
primary education at the Happy Hill R.C. School
and the J.W. Fletcher Memorial School. He went on
to the Presentation Brothers College (PBC) then to
the University of the West Indies, Cave Hill
Campus, where he gained a Bachelor of Science
Degree in Mathematics and Chemistry (1971),
followed by a Masters from Howard University
(1975) and a Doctorate in Mathematics and
Statistics from the American University (1979).

An avid player, Dr. Mitchell was a member
of the Grenada Cricket Team from 1964 – 1966. In
1973 he was made Captain of the Grenada Cricket
Team as well as the combined Windward and
Leeward Youth Team. He taught at PBC and was a
Mathematics Professor at Howard University
between 1977 and 1983. He also started a
consulting firm in Washington, D.C.

On June 20, 1995, Dr. Mitchell successfully led the party to victory in the general election, winning eight out of fifteen seats in the House of Representatives; Dr. Mitchell took office as Prime Minister on June 22, 1995.

In the 1999 election, Dr. Mitchell led the New National Party to an unprecedented victory, winning all 15 constituencies and being the first Prime Minister since Independence to win two consecutive general elections. His portfolio included Minister of National Security, Finance, Trade, Industry, Planning and Information and later on National Security and Information.

Dr. Mitchell led the Party to another unprecedented but narrowly won election on November 27, 2003, when the Party was elected to a third consecutive term in Office. He held the portfolios of National Security, Human Resource Development, Information, Information Communication Technology (ICT), Business and Private Sector Development and Youth Development. Her Majesty the Queen appointed him to the Privy Council on February 20, 2004.

The New National Party was defeated in the general election held on July 8, 2008, by the National Democratic Congress (NDC), winning only four seats against 11 for the NDC. Dr. Mitchell himself was re-elected to his seat for St. George

Northwest and continued as NNP leader. He was sworn in as Leader of the Opposition on July 16, 2008.

In his capacity as Prime Minister, Dr. Mitchell has served as Chairman of the Caribbean Community (CARICOM) from January to July 1998 and from July to December 2004; Chairman of the Board of Governors of the Caribbean Development Bank from May 1997 to May 1998; Chairman of the Ministerial Council of Association of Caribbean States from 1996 to 1997; Chairman of the Organization of Eastern Caribbean States (OECS) from May 2000 to January 2002, being the longest serving Chairman of the regional sub-group; Chairman of the Regional Security System (RSS) from April 2001 to March 2002.

Fast forward to February 19, 2013, Dr. Mitchell and his New National Party defeated the incumbent Tillman Thomas and the National Democratic Congress, winning all 15 Seats—the second time he and his party achieved such a historic feat. On February 20, 2013, Dr. The Right Honorable Keith Mitchell was sworn in as Prime Minister, for the fourth time.

He also served as the Minister of Information, Implementation, National Security, Disaster Management and Home Affairs.

Chapter Sixteen
Inclusion of Women in His Administration

Keith Mitchell has respected and admired the many invaluable contributions of women. Growing up, his mother's presence was deeply meaningful and necessary to his development as a leader as he often shares. In his administration, women have been revered in much the same way. They are called upon to participate in national leadership and decision-making at the highest levels. In the history of Grenada's politics and governance, the record shows that Keith Mitchell has made it clear that women's role in governance is an imperative to the success of our nation.

An examination of the achievements in policy formation, despite many challenges, shows that under the leadership of Keith Mitchell, implementation of the Beijing declaration and platform for action has been impressive. The Grenada National Beijing+20 review of 2014, stated that in terms of realizing and enabling an environment for gender equality in Grenada, the status of women in public life, signals that some significant strides have been made towards realizing a critical mass of women as high-level public servants.

129

This elevation of women in public life is in step with the educational pursuit of women. Under Keith Mitchell's leadership, Grenada stood fifth among the world's nations with female representatives in parliament. Approximately, 46.7% of Grenada's parliament is women. In 2014 the corps of Permanent Secretaries, who supervise respective government ministries, was predominantly women with 14 of the 17 Permanent Secretaries being women.

It should not go un-noticed that the honorable Prime Minister of Grenada appointed the first female Minister of Foreign Affairs, the distinguished Honorable Dr. Clarice Modeste-Curwen.

Grenadians should not be surprised if a female Prime Minister emerges from these very able ministers in Keith Mitchell's political reign. Women engaged in the administration of government in Grenada start at the highest level of Governor General, Her Excellency Dame Cécile La Grenade, Head of State. An impressive list of women who have served in Parliament during NNP administrations bears witness. These include Honourable Leslie-Ann Seon, who served at President of the Senate. Following are MPs elected to the House of Representatives under the NNP:

Honourable Yolande Bain–Horsford

Honourable Claris Charles
Honourable Grace Duncan
Honourable Brenda Hood
Honourable Kate Lewis
Honourable Dr. Clarice Modeste–Curwen
Honourable Kindra Maturine–Stewart
Honourable Pamela Moses
Honourable Emmalin Pierre
Honourable Delma Thomas
Honourable Laurina Waldron

In addition, almost all of Grenada's overseas embassies and missions, the most demanding posts were headed by women during his administrations. I believe this is precedent setting, and again, reveals Mitchell's break with the tradition of appointing male dominant ambassadors. I warmly congratulated the appointment of H.E. Yolande Smith, as Ambassador of Grenada to the United States and Permanent Representative to the Organization of American States (OAS). She presented her credentials to the President of the United States of America, at a most invigorating time in the relationship between Grenada and the countries of the Caribbean Community, and the USA. Her knowledge of the post, and her Washington, D.C. orientation, served well in her undertaking.

***

It is a time when policymakers and implementers are highly distracted. They are engaged in matters of national interest, in the USA, the Caribbean Community and most other jurisdictions. The treaty obligations ambassadors of the Caribbean Community should be mindful of, are the shared responsibilities they have for the coordination of effective external policy within the region. While individual country mandates may supersede, the value of collaboration must be borne in mind; circumstances should not be allowed to constrain unity. Respecting regional obligations is a hallmark of Keith Mitchell's philosophy.

However, in this new era of diplomacy, which unfolds regionally, globally, on bilateral and multilateral fronts, there are several confronting matters. Notwithstanding these issues, it is admirable to see that Grenada placed its representation abroad, in the capable hands of a new cohort of ambassadors; and particularly, in the known boiling points of diplomatic relations such as: USA, China, the United Nations, United Kingdom, and Brussels—jurisdictions of which I have learned some things.

Prime Minister Mitchell sent a clear message that our diplomatic functions were at a different level, beyond traditional styles. This new dimension of diplomatic engagement was aimed at producing serious purposeful outcomes, driven by action-oriented voices of representation, with Grenadian women at the helm

Attention must be paid to the fact that in the administration of the New National Party (NNP), under Mitchell, there has been active utilization of the rich mindsets of Grenadian women at all levels. As my late mother would say, "That makes Grenada a smart country—it knows what women can do."

The inclusion of women in nation building must not go unnoticed—especially in Keith Mitchell's government. Women were positioned to make important contributions not simply because they are women, but rather well qualified Grenadian citizens fully capable and ready for leadership.

Chapter Seventeen
Thinking Ahead Un-deterred

Sometimes while looking for answers, we trust those who may not have trust in themselves, or worst yet, have self-serving motives with the trust we placed in them. At times, their actions may be disappointing—especially when those actions do not bring the desired results many expected. Still, we must press on. Above all, while we are in the business of looking for answers, we must not prejudge any source before objective scrutiny. The final assessment of all that transpired generally brings forth the right conclusion.

*Keith Claudius Mitchell in
thoughtful reflection.*

135

In the photo above, a very revealing expression comes to Dr. Mitchell's face, which at times is quite opposite to his words. However, one thing is for sure: Keith Claudius *will* confront his critics in defense of his honor. And because he hates to make a mistake, he is never afraid to try.

When foreign investors deceive the country and fail to honor their commitments, blame is laid on our leaders for the action or inaction of external forces. When Canada discontinued visa free travel, the truth that prompted such a decision, was ignored. Yet, blame was placed on Mitchell. When the Organization for Economic Cooperation and Development (OECD) blacklisted Grenada, Mitchell was blamed for that too, and his fully legitimate effort to raise revenue, was ignored by the opposition. There is a list of unwarranted slanders that have been leveled against Mitchell. However, it is easy to see that the art of putting down a person to promote oneself is low politics, barren of ideas and weak in character.

***

Prime Minister Mitchell seamlessly moves from UN meetings, to then graciously chatting with Grenadians. Keith Mitchell is always ready to dialogue with those interested in helping Grenada.

For instance, when standing with the President of Medgar Evers University, Mitchell reminded President Rudolph Crew that Grenadians and Caribbean people continue to make valuable contributions to that institution and the City of New York.

For Keith Mitchell taking a picture with ministers and strangers is not about status, but about purpose and outcomes to follow. Few will forget his 'Silver Sands' promise and the turning of the soil, which appeared on his Christmas greeting card to the nation. He delivered in record time.

Prime Minister invites collaboration between T.A Marryshow Community College (TAMCC) in Grenada and Medgar Evers, reminding President Crew that Grenada welcomes every scholarship accommodation Medgar Evers can give a young Grenadian. The academician in Mitchell wastes no time to introduce his ambassador as being responsible for following through. Keith Mitchell remains proactive when it comes to identifying resources for Grenada and he is unabashed about pleading for his country.

Moving very confidently, he reminds the Dean of the School of Education that he looks forward to an engagement between TAMCC and Medgar Evers.

137

Mention has been made of his healthy sense of humor. What's more, Mitchell has a passion for good Grenadian and Caribbean calypso and soca music. It does not take long for him to be up on the floor and rocking. Mitchell loves to dance. It will be long remembered when Mitchell gave supporters a celebratory triumph dance to show satisfaction and gratitude for victory at the poles on March 13, 2018.

There are several memorable moments when Dr. Keith Mitchell celebrates the success of Grenadians. I recall when the Prime Minister allowed a proud mother to present her daughter who excelled in academics to be Crowned Miss Grenada among the young people in New York with Grenadian and Caribbean Heritage.

His presence, and listening ears, are a demonstration of his elation to learn of the success of persons with Grenadian parentage. This sort of knowledge moves Keith Mitchell and he takes the time to encourage and congratulate young, and old alike, who have excelled in the diaspora. Prime Minister Mitchell often refers to the work of notable Grenadians like Cisley Mason, as a person who motivates and nurtures the best in the young women of Caribbean heritage. Her Grenadian roots, he says, makes him proud. She is a force for good in the Caribbean American community.

Keith Mitchell appreciates hard workers and

encourages his colleagues to take time to assimilate and hurdle with the people. Leaders of the region consider Dr. Mitchell a man "to go to" because of his extensive experience and proactive stance on current issues. However, he does not hesitate to offer his appraisal of the situation facing the Caribbean region and its impact on the efforts of each country for sustainable economic growth.

Keith Mitchell recognizes the importance of regional unity and frequently applauds the efforts of the OECS sub region as the way forward for the wider Caribbean Community.

"We must build on our cricket legacy and continue to build sector by sector," he once said. I could not agree more. By realizing the wide scope of benefits to be derived from harnessing talent wrapped in rich young minds that emerge from Grenada, we will continue to prosper nationally. For far too long, brilliant young people have been siphoned to the North and now the East.

****

The persistent efforts of Keith Mitchell to open more space for our young people on all fronts in Grenada and the region are admirable. As Grenada moves forward in transition to a new political landscape, one must believe that those who have recently aligned themselves with the NNP are not doing so simply anticipating Mitchell's next step. They are doing so only for their personal rise to power.

It is very clear that Grenada needs its people. Those who step forward for public service must emulate Keith Mitchell. Serving oneself when the public trust is granted is unacceptable. The days when certain names and classes of people portrayed themselves as the *rightful* heirs to national leadership are over.

The appointments Keith Mitchell made have gone a long way in ensuring that the rich minds of poor Grenadians are recognized. He has done so by introducing a wide range of training and scholarship opportunities obtained by his administrations. Furthermore, Keith has made it known, that public service in Grenada cannot be self-service.

A person's work is their character in action. It is refreshing to watch Keith Mitchell in action. There is pure affection displayed in the way he shows interest in people. There is something about his smile. When he enters he reaches into the crowd and embraces people,—first with his smile, and then with his laugh. Still, Keith remains very astute about the character of the people around him. When he is not familiar with someone who is being introduced by another, he will always ask, "How *well*

140

you know that person?"

This question is usually posed whenever he gets an uneasy feeling in the presence of someone. His face will show that his intuition senses something is amiss and his smile quickly fades.

Equally important, the Prime Minister acts as if he is getting an award when mingling with Grenadians, and friends of Grenada, in his travels. In many ways, he is. The reward is seeing firsthand, the impact Grenada has made on the world. It energizes him, and he is humbled and grateful for the opportunities to serve Grenada in a meaningful way.

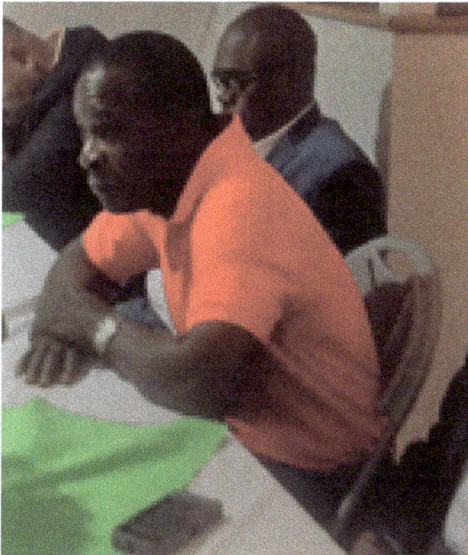

Leader Keith Mitchell,
listens at a meeting. in NY.

When around his people, it is like he is back in island space. His smile lights up the room, he becomes relaxed, and then he joins us—truly joins us. For those unfamiliar with Keith Mitchell, if you're sharing the same room, it might be hard to tell who the Prime Minister is. His ability to move from informal to formal posture is impressive. He gives the proper reverence to every situation, and values every host that has extended the invitation to have him as a guest.

His relationships with the leaders of the Caribbean Community at all levels are one of respect and pleasantry. He is a senior statesman whose wisdom is called upon. He credits his mother for teaching him to have the respect he exhibits.

It is easy to see the comfort Keith Mitchell has in the presence of people. He would be the first to tell you, that to succeed, you must know how to treat people.

Nevertheless, be mindful of the reality that you may not be treated by others the same way you treat them. There is special interest that Keith Mitchell shows in foreign nationals who demonstrate goodwill to the country.

Working with Keith Mitchell for Grenada and watching him for so many years, none of us may fully comprehend the pressures and burdens that our leaders carry.

After shaking hands, taking photos, delivering speeches, forging new partnerships, meeting world leaders, working with staff, building teams, collaborating on new policies, and everything else in-between, do they get a moment's rest? Or do they still wonder, in those moments of solitude, "Did I make the right decision? Will my people be, okay?" I imagine every leader ponders these things, because they are the ones who must shoulder the responsibilities and inconveniences. Nonetheless, when we remember that our leaders are people, like you and me, grace should be given. Remembering that in the end, they are trying their best.

In the case of Keith C. Mitchell, who holds up the mantel of service to Grenada for so many decades, I can attest, as his friend and colleague, that Keith is committed to doing his absolute best for Grenada.

Thank you for your hard work and unyielding commitment to the people Grenada, Carriacou and Petite Martinique. Your impact is indelible.

A TRIP DOWN MEMORY LANE

Cheerful acknowledgement at the podium.

145

PM Keith Mitchell speaking to constituents
You get the point.

PM Keith Mitchell with Citizen Dunbar G.
Debellotte, NY.

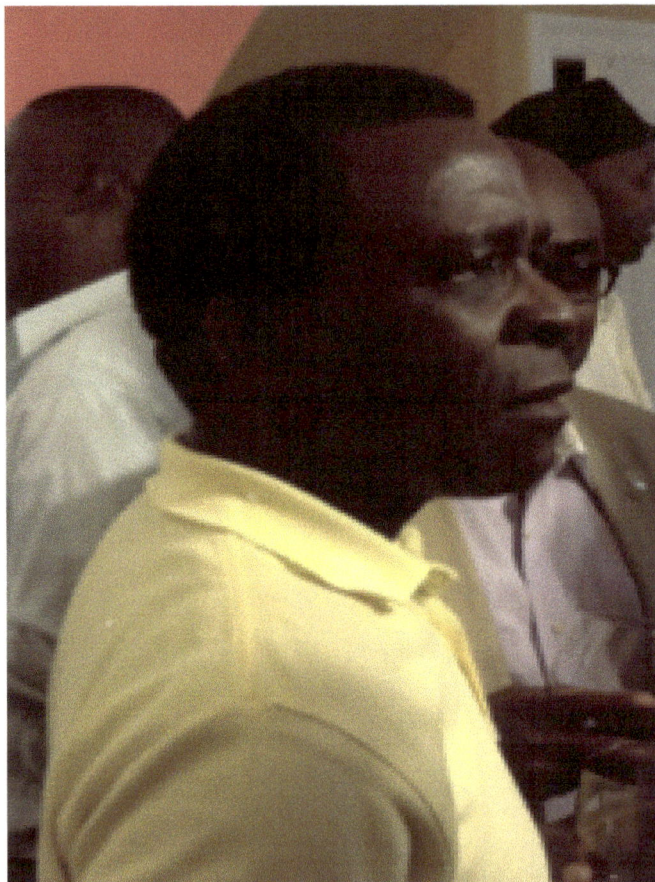

PM Keith Mitchell at a gathering in New York.

PM Keith Mitchell meeting with foreign friends

PM pondering

PM Keith Mitchell in a welcoming stance in his office.

PM greeted by Chief of Protocol and USA
Ambassador to OAS.

Crowd celebrates victory.

PM delivering a speech to the people of Grenada.

Keith Mitchell waits to be called to the podium at UN Headquarters.

Keith Mitchell celebrates with supporters.

PM arriving at town-hall meeting in NY.

*Keith Mitchell speaks to community
about important issues.*

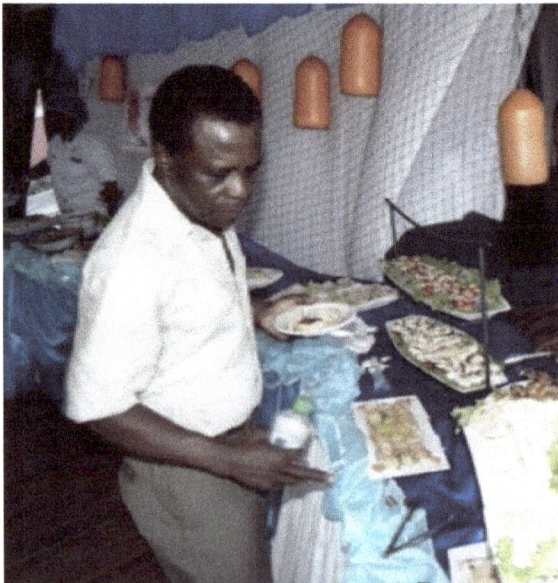

Keith Mitchell supports local vendors.

PM Keith Mitchell, Ambassador Dr. Denis Antoine, and Ambassador Schonfeld.

Friend and colleague of PM, Crepin M. Mahop.

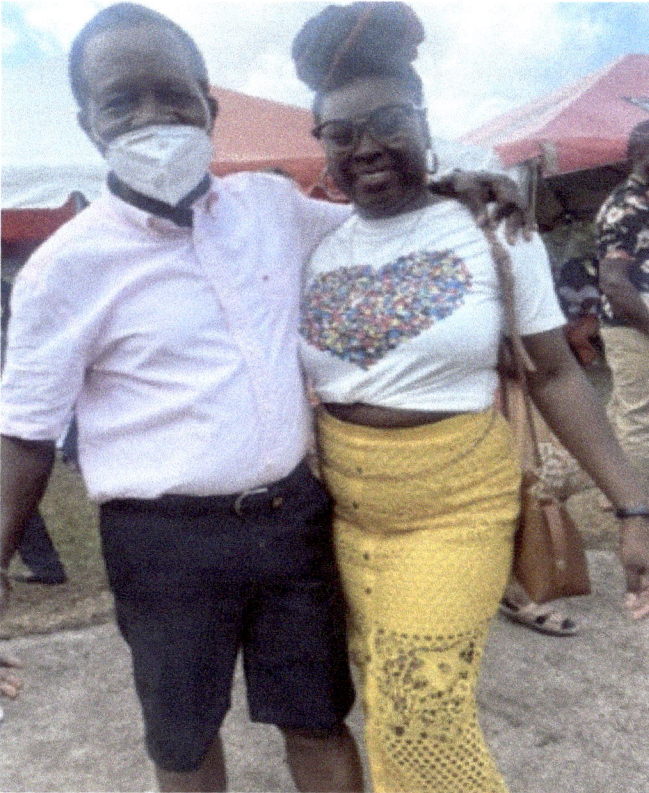

PM pauses for a photo with citizen Anika Duncan.

Keith Mitchell chats with his friend Vaughn Haynes.

Keith Mitchell with former roommate/Dentist,
Dr. Wilfred Charles

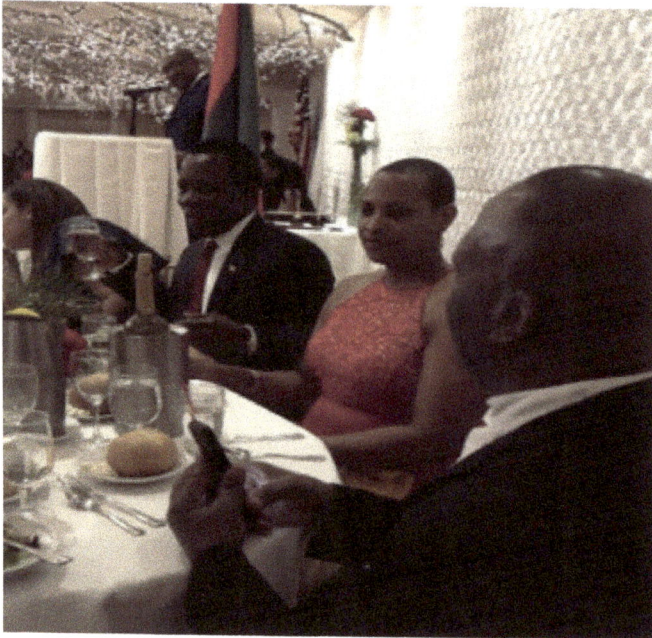

*Dinner with Ambassadors at
Independence Gala in NYC.*

*Prime Minister in Consultation on
the floor of the UN General Assembly.*

A genuine Keith Mitchell smile.

A NOTE OF THANKS

Thank you, Dr. the Hon. Keith C. Mitchell. After more than twenty-five years of privileged front line diplomatic service before the international community for Grenada, it is with a sense of humility and gratitude, that I say thank you for having placed confidence and trust in me, to be appointed as Grenada's diplomatic representative for so many years—in so many responsible positions.

I am very pleased to have served Grenada selflessly, fearlessly, and faceless to many Grenadians, who have never seen or noticed who I am, having served out of the country.

I joined the foreign service of Grenada following my service in Grenada in the Ministry of Health, as a Malaria Evaluator and emerging health inspector. Following my travel to the United States, I remained involved in the affairs of Grenada from abroad after graduation from college.

After serving as Counsellor Alternate Representative at Embassy/Permanent Mission of Grenada to the Organization of American States (OAS) from 1987-1990 in Washington D.C., then being called back to the Embassy as Grenada's Ambassador to the United States and the OAS in 1995; I reflect on how things were when I started compared to Grenada today, and I smile with some degree of satisfaction that I may have done something along the way that contributed to the growth and strength of Grenada in the present day.

I wish also to acknowledge the members of the Prime Minister's Cabinet who supported the Prime Minister by consenting to my service as Ambassador. With God as my guide, and driven by my desire and commitment to make a contribution,

166

I have worked with the understanding that I had to brighten the corner entrusted to the authority vested in me.

Throughout my years of service, I strove to do one thing—make my space better than when it was delegated to me. Like a professional house painter, a vocation I am proud of, during my tenure I have colored and painted the walls of construction designated to me, in the vision of the architect of modern Grenada, Keith Claudius Mitchell.

Dr. Mitchell, thank you, for your inspiration, which motivated my determination to give without any reservation, committed only to the fact that you have modeled the same character of loyalty for the good of Grenada. I have remained emboldened, and faithful, by the realization that nowadays Grenada has become a household name, not for coup d'état, but as one of the safest places in the world, known throughout the globe, as one of the most exciting places on earth to visit, acclaimed for exemplar leadership in fiscal management, and stellar contribution to address the challenge of climate change.

The world admires the celebration of our peaceful electoral procedure, good governance and our command voice of representation, in global political fora. In addition, the achievements of young Grenadians in higher education, sports, science, culture, and all other walks of life, are celebrated. The increases in the number international visitors to Grenada as tourists and investors, are added indicators that the country is led along the right path to sustainable development. My journey from Beauregard in Birch Grove to the world stage broadened when I met Keith Claudius Mitchell along the way, and he took notice, and I too observed in him, an inexorable willpower to offer himself for larger service for our country. I am pleased to have followed and served.

You have my continued support of your vision for Grenada. I wish you sustained good health and God's blessings.

And thank you Dr. Mitchell, for helping me to learn and accept It is not easy…

To apologize, To begin over, To be unselfish,
To take advice, to admit error, to face a sneer
To be charitable, to keep trying
To be considerate, to avoid mistakes, to endure success
To profit by mistakes, to forgive and forget
To think and then act, to keep out of a rut
To make the best of little, to subdue an unruly temper
To shoulder a deserved blame, to recognize a silver lining
It always pays.

PM Keith Mitchell doing the dance with rhythm from within.

www.ingramcontent.com/pod-product-compliance
Lightning Source LLC
Chambersburg PA
CBHW041821090426
42811CB00009B/1057